GARDENS OF LONGEVITY

PIERRE AND SUSANNE RAMBACH

GARDENS OF LONGEVITY

IN CHINA AND JAPAN

The Art of the Stone Raisers

SKIRA

RIZZOLI
NEW YORK

© 1987 by Editions d'Art Albert Skira S.A., Geneva.

Published in the United States of America in 1987 by

RIZZOLI INTERNATIONAL PUBLICATIONS, INC.
597 Fifth Avenue/New York 10017

Translated from the French by André Marling

ISBN 0-8478-0837-8

Printed in Switzerland

CONTENTS

THE STONES 7

    The art of the stone raisers 8
    The Gardens of Longevity 14
    Peking, Yangzhou and Suzhou 16
    Destruction and continuity 20
    Longevity and Breath Force 20
    Breath Force and works of art 24
    Dreamstones and Breath Force 27

STONES AND THE EMPEROR 31

    The imperial progress 32
    Axis-of-the-world stones 33
    Fantastic stones 38

EMPEROR AND DRAGONS 43

    The dance of the dragons 44
    Dragon shapes on the land mass of China . . . 48
    The dragon cycle 50

MAN AND DRAGONS 53

    The descent of the dragon 54
    The dragon drivers 58
    The dragon's lair 60
    The manipulation of sites 66
    The mountain and its double 74

MAN AND STONES 79

    The scholar in his garden 80
    Closed spaces and distant views 84
    Movements and angles of vision 88
    Paving of assembled waters 92

THE GREAT RULE OF
THE METAMORPHOSIS OF THE WORLD . . 95

    Fleeting spring 96
    Summer mountains 100
    Autumn walks 108
    Winter visions 113

NEAR STONES, FAR MOUNTAINS 117

    The poet forsaken by the nymph 118
    Climbing the mountain 119
    The mountain contemplated 124

THE MOVEMENT OF STONES 129

    Clouds carve mountains 130
    The Isles of the Immortals 140
    The cosmic dance 146

THE OMNIPRESENT SEA 153

    Crystallization 154
    Imported dragons 156
    From Chang'an to Kyōto 158
    The stones of the prince 160
    The stones of the seashore 162
    Sign and form 166

THE WAY OF THE STONES 171

    Ongoing doctrines 172
    The stone-bound instant 176
    The stones of the Chan monasteries 178
    Images of the universe 180

PAINTINGS TRANSPOSED 183

    The waterfall and the island 184
    The three planes of the landscape 186

ART AND LONGEVITY 195

    Chinese philosophy, Japanese perception . . . 196
    Three, five, seven stones 200
    The message of the Gardens of Longevity . . . 204

DEDICATION 210

Notes 211
List of Gardens 215
Bibliography 217
List of Illustrations 219
Index 225
Acknowledgments 231

THE STONES

Suzhou: Garden of the Master of the Fishing Nets (Wangshiyuan).

The art of the stone raisers

Suzhou: Garden of the Master of the Fishing Nets. Overall view of the north-west courtyard in front of the Late Spring Studio. This courtyard was reconstructed in the Astor Court at the Metropolitan Museum of Art, New York.

Detail on the opposite page.

Since 1981 the art of the stone raisers has officially made its entry into the world of the museum. In the spring of that year, in the Metropolitan Museum of Art in New York a new room, Astor Court, was arranged as a garden in order to make an original kind of rest room and a typical setting for a collection of Ming dynasty furniture. The stones raised in this room come from the Suzhou region and were put in place by Chinese experts in the restoration of gardens.

This recognition of stone raising—generally deemed a lesser skill by historians of Western art who barely give it a mention—does not mean that it is now considered an art in its own right, like architecture, painting or sculpture. Nevertheless, as will be seen in this work, in some ages it was one of the chosen modes of expression of creative artists in both China and Japan.

It is no doubt because this art was practised longest in China that the stone compositions still to be seen there today are not very old. In the course of the years most of them have been remade or transformed by the successive owners of the palace or residence gardens where they are found.

It is known, for example, that the Garden of the Master of the Fishing Nets (Wangshiyuan) in Suzhou—a small part of which is reproduced in Astor Court—was built in the twelfth century, but was a ruin in the fifteenth. It was, however, entirely remade at the end of the eighteenth century and renovated again in the course of the nineteenth and twentieth centuries.

In Japan, on the other hand, many stone compositions created between the fourteenth and seventeenth centuries, not in private homes but in Buddhist monasteries, were the work of founder abbots of the monasteries or great artists who stayed in them. Held to convey messages and a teaching whose meaning was liable to be changed by any alteration, they were carefully kept in their original form until the beginning of the twentieth century.

From the time of the Meiji Revolution in 1868, the Japanese, in order to be able to master Western technologies, began to study forms of expression

Compositions by Mirei Shigemori.

1 Kyōto: Daitoku-ji Zen Monastery, 1961.
   Mount Horai in front of the Zuiho-in tea house.

2 Kishiwada Castle (Osaka Prefecture), 1953.
   The group of stones represent generals surrounded
   by their staff.

10

3 Kyōto: Garden of the Tōfuku-ji Zen Monastery, 1938-1939.

alien to their culture. The traditional arts, already losing their vitality, sank into decadence for lack of any interest in them. As recently as the 1950s, teachers at the Tokyo Landscape School gave as an example of gardens the public parks in big German cities. As for composition in stone, this art would have been almost wholly forgotten if Mirei Shigemori, born in 1896, had not vowed to himself, about 1920, that he would revive it. Before his thirtieth year, he had travelled the length and breadth of his country in search of old gardens and published a survey of them in 27 volumes. He then began restoring the abandoned gardens of the Kyōto monasteries. In 1938-1939 he made the stone compositions of the Tōfuku-ji Zen monastery in the purest Zen tradition, and in 1961, one in the tea-pavilion garden of the Zuiho-in monastery in the Daitoku-ji complex at Kyōto. He renewed the art of stone raising, adapting it to contemporary settings, as in the garden of Kishiwada Castle.

During the same period, great architects included stone compositions in their modern buildings, such as Kenzō Tange for Takamatsu Town

Hall, or Tom Hatashita, a Canadian of Japanese origin, who after studying for five years with Mirei Shigemori, made gardens in India, Paris and Zaïre, before going back to work in Toronto; also sculptors like Isamu Noguchi, a Japanese American born in 1904, who made gardens and stone compositions in Japan, Paris (for the UNESCO building) and New York (for the Chase Manhattan Bank).

The researches of a few lone artists have thus brought back the centuries-old art of stone raising, after a temporary decline, as a mode of expression for Japanese artists.

In China most of the gardens have weathered ill the far-reaching social changes that have taken place since the end of the nineteenth century. As the age of crises fades into the past, they are coming into their own again. Year by year, a growing number of gardens are being faithfully restored. At the same time, original stone compositions are also beginning to be made, that is to say compositions no longer copied from old models but drawing more directly on the deepest sources of Chinese culture. Stone compositions have left the garden of the scholar or the Emperor for the public sector and are sometimes found in public gardens, in front of government buildings, or in the gardens of hotels, and not always hotels for foreign guests. It is heartening to see that the old fascination of stones for the Chinese is far from dying out. When, however, we asked Mr Chen Congzhou, Professor of the history of architecture at Tongji University in Shanghai, whether, in China as in Japan, artists today also express themselves in stone compositions, he replied—too modestly for us to be able to believe him altogether—that "the time had not yet come to seek new expressions, it was necessary first of all to concentrate on the study and restoration of the works of the past."

What he said was only an echo, crossing the centuries, of the words of the author of the *Sakutei-ki*, who began his treatise:

"When you raise stones... you must study the old traditional art of the garden by going to see the finest examples."

Takamatsu (Shikoku Island): Composition by the architect Kenzō Tange for the Town Hall.

Suzhou: Modern composition in the garden of a hotel.

12

Peking: Composition of 1984 in front of the Qiaoyuan Hotel.

Peking: Stones raised along a byway of Chang'an Avenue.

Peking, Beihai Park: Contemporary arrangement outside the former Retreat of the Painted Boat (Huafangzhai).

The Gardens of Longevity

The *Sakutei-ki* (Notes on the making of gardens), known also by the name *Zen sai hisho* (Summary of the secrets of garden construction), is a calligraphed scroll dating from the end of the twelfth century. The presumed author, Yoshitsune Gokyōhoko, who died in 1206, appears to have included in it parts of a work written in 1040 and attributed to Yoshitsuna Tachibana. The *Sakutei-ki* is to date the oldest known treatise on the construction of gardens.

Like all professional works, the *Sakutei-ki* seems a closed book to the uninitiated; that is why in Japan it is even today only known to garden specialists. The oral transmission of knowledge from masters to their followers was still the general rule in many disciplines until the nineteenth century. In the case of gardens, their layout being linked with cosmic harmony, special safeguards surrounded the spread of knowledge concerning them.

The *Sakutei-ki* was therefore a secret handbook meant to remind confirmed masters of gardens of already ancient traditions (perhaps then being lost). It has appeared to us also, in the course of our work, to have borne witness to the new trend, compared with the Chinese archetype, that was then taking shape.

When we wrote *The Secret Book of Japanese Gardens* (published in 1973) we tried, by glossing a text, to bring to light the elements of the "general theory of gardens" referred to by the author without any further explanation in the first sentence of his manuscript: "When you raise stones, you must remember the general theory of gardens."

Reversing the proposition, this amounts to saying that a garden without stones would not have the name garden. This would appear to mean that the main substance of the treatise was to be concerned with the rules for the choice and arrangement of the stones.

In the last chapter, dealing with the art of planting and springs, veiled hints are finally given of the elements of this theory, namely the purpose of the garden:

— To recreate symbolically ideal surroundings in which man can have his being and live happily.

— To be a vision of the "Pure Land" of Buddha Amida, the cosmic unity of the one who has reached Awakening.

— To enable man, following up his meditation, to go ahead along the road of spiritual search leading to Awakening.

— To ease the descent of the tutelary spirits.

— To be a micro-image of Japan, identified as the Isles of the Immortals of Chinese tradition.

— To rouse fine feelings through the recreation of a "Japan space" peopled by divinities, suitable for the celebration of a cult to the beauty of the world.

As these aims are set forth, there is no ground for listing them in any hierarchical order of importance; each of them being age-old, all that matters is the whole they form together. The stress laid by the author in naming Japan gives three of them the appearance of having been native to that country; nevertheless, in view of some of the ideas they echo, they could be equally well linked with a Chinese origin. The second part of this work will deal precisely with the way this origin was in some sort obviated so as to make it easier to fit them to another context.

If the reference to Japan is set aside, the same aims can then be seen, either openly expressed or glimpsed below the surface, in Chinese gardens. Each of them seems to us like a sixfold repetition of the same search: the physical and spiritual search, pursued singly or in common, for LONGEVITY; which the garden could be one means among others of attaining.

Peking, Forbidden City: Garden of the Palace of Tranquil Longevity (Ningshougong).

Peking, Yangzhou and Suzhou

Over 80% of Japanese gardens are concentrated in the region of Kyōto, which remained the imperial capital and the foremost cultural and political centre of the country down to 1868—that is, for more than a thousand years. Not so in China. There the capital was continually being moved in keeping with dynastic changes. At many places imperial palaces were built, then abandoned; the same is true, in their wake, of aristocratic residences and the homes of scholar-officials.

For the late twentieth century traveller who may wish to visit the Gardens of Longevity and finds to his surprise that a flight of a thousand miles separates the two main centres where they are concentrated (i.e. Peking, Yangzhou and the Suzhou region), we shall give some brief and essential particulars; these he can extend and complete by further reading. However, to help him to keep his bearings in the immense sweep of China in both space and time, as also in the succession of Japanese dynasties and periods of history, we provide a bookmark which will serve the reader for ready reference and spare the writers from adding a plethora of historical details.

Political and cultural powers were usually centralized in the capital city. But when Peking became the imperial capital in 1420, a cleavage occurred between the court established there and the whole of the scholarly elite which remained concentrated further south. The Gardens of Longevity to be seen in Peking today are mostly those built by the Emperors.

The founding of the cities of Yangzhou and Suzhou goes back to the fifth century B.C., to the time of Confucius and Laozi. At that time there already existed a connecting canal prefiguring the Grand Canal dug in the sixth century A.D. Later, throughout the Sui dynasty, a network of navigable waterways was built, formed of canals and rivers linking the valleys of the Huanghe (Yellow River) and the Wei with those of the Jiangzi (Blue River) in its lower reaches as far as Yangzhou.

The starting point of the Grand Canal, Yangzhou in the Tang period was a great seaport for ships travelling to Korea, Japan, Canton and India. From there in 753 A.D. sailed the monk Jianzhen, whom the Japanese call Ganjin. He and his companions carried to Japan, in addition to 3,000 Buddhist relics, the architectural skills of Tang China and the art of stone compositions.

In 838 A.D. the Japanese monk Ennin landed at Yangzhou. In the account of his long voyage he mentioned the presence there of forty Buddhist monasteries. Marco Polo, in the service of Qubilai from 1275 to 1291, was put in charge of the administration of this trading city for three years.

In 1645, one year after the fall of the Ming dynasty, the population of Yangzhou was exterminated by the Manchu troops, but the city recovered rapidly and prospered once more: it was at that time one of the principal centres of culture. Merchants who had grown rich in the salt trade built themselves sumptuous residences or bought up the homes of the scholars; they supported many artists, including the painter Shitao (also known by the name of Daozi), author of a treatise entitled *Remarks on Painting by the Monk Bitter Pumpkin*. A few years ago a garden laid out by Shitao was rediscovered in Yangzhou.

Once an important transhipping centre, Yangzhou, which had to withstand the Taiping rebellion from 1857 to 1863, is today, with its population of 370,000, a modest provincial city. Of its past splendours there subsist quite remarkable stone compositions, chiefly in the private gardens of Geyuan, Heyuan and Xiaopangu, as well as in the Buddhist monastery Daming.

Suzhou, situated west of Shanghai, is much better known than Yangzhou; it is par excellence the city of scholars' gardens, of very ancient origin. Specialists place the creation of some of them in the tenth century, but those that can be seen today hardly existed in their present form before the sixteenth. Of two hundred gardens listed in 1949, only

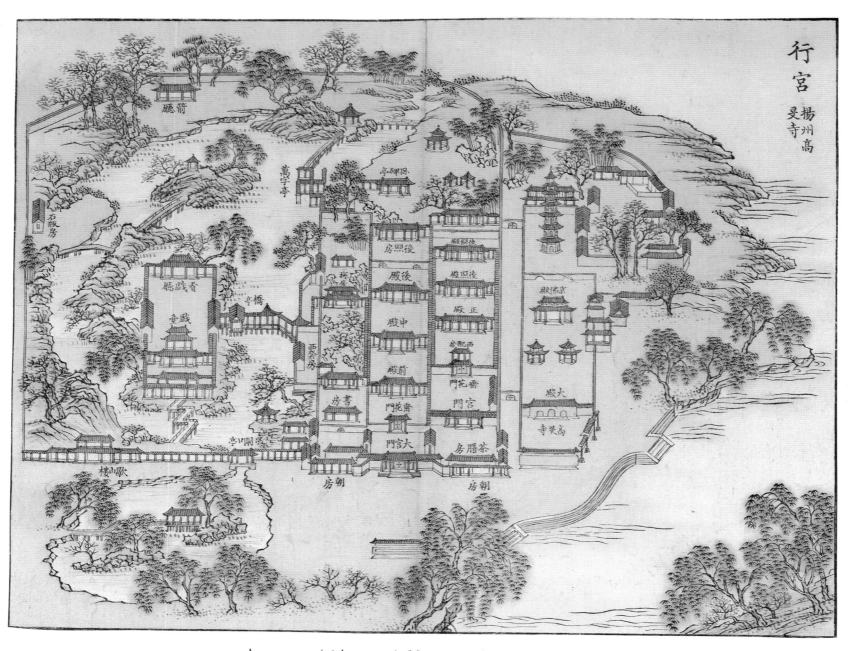

Anonymous (18th century): Monastery of the Great Bright Temple
(Daming si) at Yangzhou, whose first abbot in the 8th century was the monk Jianzhen.
Plate from the album *Palaces of the Emperor along the Road*
from Peking to Suzhou, six or seven leagues from each other.

nine are now completely restored and open to the public: they are the most important ones. From ancient records we know that the old part of the city today has changed little in its structure since the sixth century B.C., when it was the capital of the state of Wu.

In 1127 the capital of the Song dynasty was moved from Bianliang (Kaifeng) to Lin'an (Hangzhou). Together with the imperial family, all the prestigious culture of the Huanghe valley moved to the immediate proximity of Suzhou, which was then to become the favoured place of residence of administrators, nobles and scholars of the new capital. Marco Polo, on a visit there in 1275, compared it, perhaps with a certain nostalgia, to Venice. He found at Suzhou the same hump-backed bridges that span the canals crisscrossing the city; and also, no doubt, a highly refined atmosphere.

It was from Lake Tai near Suzhou, a very ancient sea whose waters had become fresh, that were

17

Peking, Summer Palace (Yiheyuan) north-west of the capital.

extracted strange white or light-coloured rocks with rounded and contoured forms, pierced by holes, which are to be found in all the stone compositions in the city gardens. Strange stones in truth: message-bearing stones, whose value must be appreciated in order to understand the fascination they exercised over so many generations. We find them in the gardens of the Forbidden City, the Beihai and the Summer Palace of Peking, transported by canal from Lake Tai. The emperors, particularly those of the Ming dynasty, continued to send emissaries to the south in search of the finest specimens, and some of these stones were "borrowed" from the gardens of Suzhou.

18

◁△ Peking, Forbidden City: Stone from Lake Tai.

Many stones from Lake Tai adorning the gardens of Suzhou were taken for the Emperor Qianlong and set up in the gardens of the Summer Palace, on the north bank of Lake Kunming, or in the gardens of the Forbidden City.

19

Destruction and continuity

Once the foundations of thought had been established in China, with the invention of script in the sixteenth century B.C., the originality of its culture could continue down to our own time, through a tumultuous history of flowerings and waves of destruction, or self-destruction. No civilization has been so conscious of its long continuance and so constant in its philosophy. Thus every territorial conquest by the tribes of "barbaric" horsemen coming from the western or northern steppes ended in the assimilation of the invaders, who, charmed by the refinement of this culture, had no concern but to adopt and extend it. Changes of system or government that had irreversible consequences for other civilizations never really did any damage to the Chinese order of things. Purges and destructions, even draconian, were never absolute; documents sent for safekeeping into exile in remote provinces were fetched back again by emissaries when the political situation had once more been stabilized, a tradition still alive a few years ago, when in 1976 the city of Tangshan was wiped out by an earthquake and rescuers discovered between the double walls of a house many writings proscribed during the destructive wave of the Cultural Revolution.

"The first Emperor, Shiko, ordered the burial of all books and scholars; but he set aside the book on the art of planting," wrote the Japanese author of the *Sakutei-ki*. He was alluding to the Burning of the Books decreed in 213 B.C. by Shi Huang di. Other sources, less restrictive, tell us that the Emperor ordered all books to be burned except treatises on medicine, agriculture and divination. But in limiting the preservation of books to those on the art of planting, our author, we believe, was not far wrong; for gardens originally had, among others, magical and propitiatory functions.

Plate from Wang Gai's
Mustard Seed Garden Manual of Painting, 1679.

Longevity and Breath Force

The word longevity should be taken in the sense of maintaining the state of youth, and not a mere prolonging of life into old age.

Already forgotten and outdated in the time of Laozi was the archaic notion that Man had appeared on earth, an earth all ready to welcome him, at the shake of a "magic wand" by some extraterrestrial Creator. A pantheistic vision of the world now led men to look to nature, of which they were an integral part, for the origin of the pulsations animating them. The fact of considering the Universe in its entirety as a living organism had prompted the Chinese quite naturally not to dissociate heaven, earth and waters, not to divide Mind from Matter, not to establish any differences between animate and inanimate. To attain longevity, men felt that.they must attune themselves to that living Universe in order to grasp its laws of equilibrium, described as Yin and Yang, and to steep themselves in the currents pulsing through earth and sky which they had to define; and did define by the sign 氣 (Qi), which will often be referred to in this book by the term Breath Force. To attain longevity, then, it was necessary to maintain within oneself as long as possible, in the best working condition, this life principle, this Breath Force, which from the earliest times appeared to philosophers to be of like nature in all the manifestations of the Universe.

Originally the sign 气 stood for a vapour; to it was later added the sign for a grain of rice 米 as a symbol of materiality and energy as opposed to the exhaled breath. It then became a sign of which these were some of the many acceptations: vapour, exhalation, gas, fluid, but also the life spirit that quickens the human body, animal spirits or humours. It is also an element of materiality entering into the composition of all things, in combination with the element 理 (li), the principle of order.

The most living of breaths, it pursues through man's body precisely defined paths (unknown to Western medicine, since they do not correspond either to the nervous or to the vascular system), into which the acupuncturist, in his treatments, inserts his needles.

The most cosmic of breaths, issuing at the same time from the sky and the depths of the earth, it courses through all nature, but with varying intensity; the more or less perceptible traces it leaves in matter seem from earliest times to have fascinated the Chinese, who set themselves to locating the points of its strongest concentration so as to saturate themselves with it, while they also sought to give it material form in symbolic decorations on the objects they fashioned, in the consciousness that a manufactured material does not have its origin in inert matter.

Peking, Forbidden City: Imperial Garden (Yuhuayuan) laid out under the Mings. Cypress trunk. Some trees in this garden are said to go back to the time of its construction.

"There are young people, grown-ups, old folks, invalids and able-bodied people, all social and professional categories mingling in a somewhat collusive anonymity. The most fascinating of these figures are perhaps those who are doing nothing, motionless as trees or stones, like apples in a Cézanne painting. In a shadowy thicket they may even be confused with trees, as if in osmosis with them, like native elements of the landscape. They are unmoving and unoccupied, as if intent on putting a stop to time, with no pretence to meditating or dozing, in order to give themselves the illusion of an assured bearing. The gaze is at once absent and present; they appear to see without looking."
(Jean-Marie Simonet)

21

Peking, Beihai Park: Unrestored outbuilding in the Serenity Study (Jingxinzhai).

In his garden, his private realm of longevity, Chinese man saw to it that the flow of these vital energies should be visible or traceable, both in the composition of the natural elements (water, stone, vegetation) and in the man-made elements (pavilions, walls, bridges, bases and lattices). In this way he was able to revitalize himself through the outflow of energies from the elements around him. To the discovery, or belief, that certain stones of peculiar shape are the chosen receivers and transmitters of this precious Breath Force, we may attribute the almost obsessive passion the Chinese have for these stones, which invariably figure in their gardens. To attain longevity, it is of the utmost importance for a man to keep his garden in good working order by unrelaxing care and upkeep. When tree growth is no longer controlled, when the flow of water dries up, and the stones are loosened and scattered, then the garden dies and man can gain no further benefit from it.

Woodcut from a painting by Qian Gu. Plate from the *Xixiangji* published during the Wanli era, Ming Dynasty, between 1573 and 1619.

Suzhou: Garden to Linger In (Liuyuan). Rock known as
the Cloud-Nestling Peak (Xiuyunfeng). See page 149.

Breath Force and works of art

Here, a man in his garden, a person of rank; the inscription specifies that he is a collector. Comfortably ensconced in an armchair very much like those still to be seen today in the residences of the Suzhou gardens (p. 27), he has asked his servants to fetch him his treasures and gazes at them. For the painter and viewers of future generations, he displays his chosen works of art as tokens of his eclectic tastes: tripod vases of the Bronze Age, perfume braziers, statues, ceramics, all of them objects from which the energy of matter seems to glow and radiate; and a servant is about to unroll before his eyes a scroll painting. He is in his garden, on a terrace which appears to overlook a stretch of water, the extension of an empty landscape from which he holds aloof, as if protecting himself. On the right side, behind a folding screen decorated with mountains, two young women are taking out the *qin*, a seven-stringed cithara, the favourite musical instrument of the Chinese scholar; and on the table are a heap of boxes containing scrolls, of painting or calligraphy, which he will be looking at by and by, unless perhaps... The painter has depicted the accumulation of objects but not the sequence of events.

Behind the man is a screen, another shelter against the emptiness beyond. It forms a hiding place, framed by motifs carved in wood, and these motifs are stereotypes of clouds. The screen stands on heavy legs. The clouds, then, have been caught and held. The screen painting is interesting: it evokes waves, mist, flying spray—the swirl of water.

Near the screen, which he is not looking at but which seems to radiate towards him, is a tree which by skilful cutting and clipping has been made to seem at least a hundred years old; its gnarled trunk and branches tell plainly of the passing and acting of vital energies.

In China art and nature have never been opposed. A stone, by the mere fact of having been picked up by a scholar, taken home by him and placed in his garden or set on a stand, becomes a work of art; so too with a shrub whose growth has been under the watchful control of an aesthete. Penjing, *known in the West under the Japanese name* bonsai, *was already considered at the Tang court, twelve centuries ago, as a full-fledged art, on a par with painting or calligraphy. Like all the arts,* penjing *has a magical role: by miniaturizing a tree, it permits a concentration of all the beneficent energies it contains.*

Suzhou: *Penjing* in the Garden of the Stupid Official (Zhuozhengyuan).

Attributed to Du Jin (later 15th century), Ming Dynasty:
Enjoying Antiquities. Silk scroll.

*The theme of the scholar admiring an antique (wangu)
is also known as bowu, which means examining or
studying antiquities. For the literati this discipline was
one way of expressing their attachment to the ritual of
the ancients.*

In this enclosed space he confronts a stone, on
which the gaze of all the figures seems to converge.
Set against a flat rock, the stone expresses the ten-
sion of energies in its shape, similar in this to the
stones in the screen painting. Tree and stone make
it clear that the scene is set in a garden. They are the
stable elements; the others are movable, transport-
able, brought here from the residence.

In this painting in an archaizing style, an interesting point to note is precisely its "genre scene"
aspect. It conveys a need for the presence of mountains, geographically more remote from the urban

residence than near it. The mountain landscape
seems to be indispensable to the man, who relies on
it to impart to him some of the energy embodied in
it. He has represented it in his garden in the form
of a stone which expresses, not the mountain mass,
but the inner currents pervading it: He has brought
it into his garden in the form of paintings: mountains as a summing up of nature.

Paintings, objects and garden also express both
the Yin/Yang principles and the representations of
the Breath Force emanating from the matter which
radiates over the spirit of man.

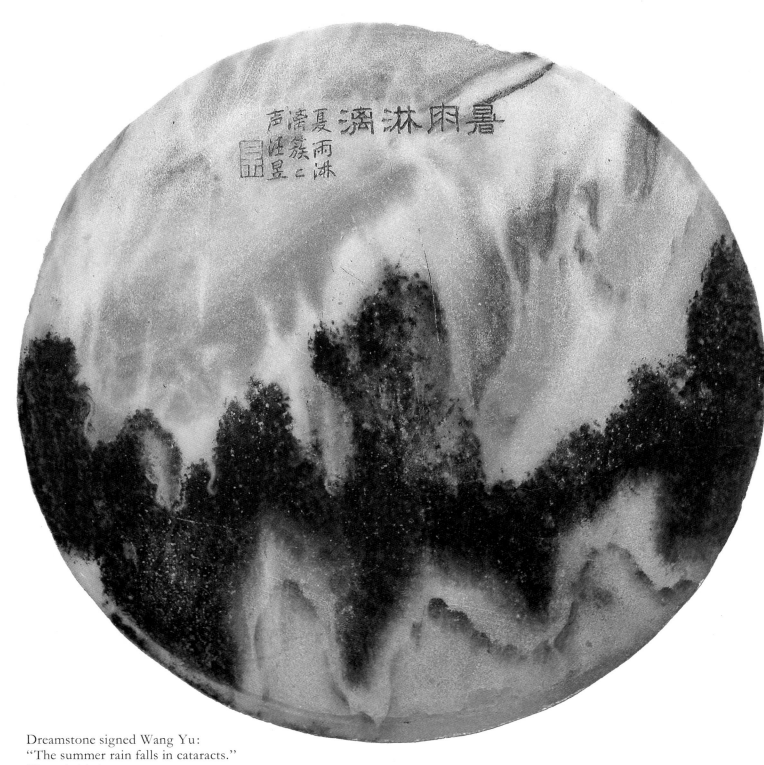

Dreamstone signed Wang Yu:
"The summer rain falls in cataracts."
The subtitle is:
"The summer rain murmurs as it falls."

Dreamstones and Breath Force

To enter the Gardens of Longevity by the contemplation of dreamstones, two-dimensional representations that do not fail to evoke the inspired calligraphies of Chinese and Japanese masters, can be a way of leaving the known; that which is familiar to us. Contemplating them is like hearing the voice projected to the far side of the mountain, an echo before it ever reaches the ears; like watching a reflection quiver in the looking-glass before having seen its subject; like holding in one's hands the nectar drop, the pearl, before it has trickled from the alembic. To gaze upon dreamstones is also to contemplate the ultimate reality of the Universe in the evocation of its energy movements which constitute Tao.

And for us, entering the Gardens of Longevity in this way will be to penetrate the Chinese cosmogony, which has pervaded all cultural levels ever since the structures of Chinese thought became firmly established.

Contemplating the dreamstones, the Chinese, imbued with Taoist philosophy, found in the petrified swirls of their veinings a perfect expression of the Breath Force, identifying them with the generic form of the mountain. And they become so exactly identified with the mountain, whose steep jags, gushing springs and banks of mist they reproduce, that they seem, more than its emanation, its concentrated form. It is said of some of them that they almost realistically evoke the mountainous landscapes of the celebrated site of Guilin.

Extracted from the marble quarries of the high plateaus of Yunnan, a remote region of the southwest on the borders of Burma and Viēt-Nam, neighbouring the mighty Himalayas, these slabs show in their veinings the traces of mineral combinations of pure limestone and sedimentary layers of clay mixed with organic material or iron oxides which the limestone has recrystallized. Preserved and inscribed in them, then, is the expression of formidable telluric energies which caused the folding of the mountains.

Was it not odd, this search for a Breath Force in such remote places? Considering the historical fortunes of the province of Yunnan, it may be conjectured that these marble slabs were originally quarried to decorate the mosques and wealthy residences of the Moslems who occupied this region about the twelfth century, when Moslem influence penetrated into China. It was to a Moslem that the Mongols entrusted the construction of their palace in Peking in the thirteenth century; and let us remember the marble inlays of St Sophia in Constantinople or of the Mosque of Omar in Jerusalem. But most probably the Chinese read other signs in these decorations, signs that touched them deeply; and thus, perhaps, they created these dreamstones.

Dreamstones. They are sometimes called journeying stones: stones of a journey for artists and aesthetes through the Taoist cosmogony, like a journey within oneself, obeying identical laws.

These stones are accessories to the Gardens of Longevity. They are to be found either framed and hanging from pavilion walls or inlaid in the back of heavy armchairs. They were unquestionably regarded as transmitters of beneficent energies. Together with screen and scroll paintings, they formed part of the home furnishings and—journeying stones in this sense too—accompanied the scholar whenever and wherever he moved.

Suzhou: Residence in the Garden of the Master of the Fishing Nets.
Dreamstone mounted on the back of an armchair.

Suzhou: Residence in the Garden of the Master of the Fishing Nets.
Dreamstones now hanging on the walls of the reception room,
originally mounted on screens.

29

Bewildered by his first sight of these stones raised to the rank of works of art, the Westerner may try to relate them to certain of his own values: one composition may be reminiscent of a Henry Moore sculpture, another of a group by Rodin. In front of others, he may be fascinated by their zoomorphic or even anthropomorphic features. And the friend or guide acquainting him with the extravagant shapes of these "lion stones" or "tiger stones" or "dragon stones," will go far to reinforce this initial interpretation of appearances which, by their very essence, are images of the Universe in its wholeness. It would indeed be surprising, before these stones, for the mentor to express the great principles of Yin and Yang, the pulses of the Earth, the course of the Breath Force. Underlying notions, these, for the stones were chosen (and are still?) for their capacity to express one aspect of the Universe, but without excluding the others.

Peking: Garden of the Summer Palace.

STONES AND THE EMPEROR

Anonymous, Song Dynasty: Breaking the Balustrade.
Detail of a silk scroll painting.

The imperial progress

Peking, Forbidden City:
Stairs leading to the Hall of Preserving Harmony (Baohe dian).

Did the Emperor, the Son of Heaven, sometimes have occasion to tread the Earth with His August Feet? Sometimes, to be sure, when he symbolically broke the ground in his field, so that the celestial seeds might fecundate it; the other occasions were more rare, except for the private sphere.

In the Forbidden City the open spaces connecting the official pavilions or separating the more private residences (both types never standing flat on the ground but always more or less elevated) consist of paved areas rather like seas or deserts, out of which arise the imperial buildings. Dignitaries and servants approach them by staircases, but the Son of Heaven never enters but by floating upwards above ramps flanked by stairs, in a flight over mythical lands. These ramps, the workmanship of which varies besides in quality, all bear the same engraved emblematic devices: flashing dragons, lands and waters in flux, cosmic pearls; all the elements of a fantastic creation brought together.

Petty or pregnant details: thus the choice of this ramp did not warrant our writing that the Emperor flew over it to take part in the rites of the Halls of Supreme Harmony, Complete Harmony and Preserving Harmony; for, following an immutable order, it marks the end of the Imperial Progress, when the Emperor had left the Supreme Heights and beneath his person unrolled once again a moment in the history of the Universe.

First came the scrolled dragons in odd-numbered compositions, combinations of three and five, joined by the central dragon who spits forth the pearl. And, his body taking on infinite extension, "He" regains his footing by five conical mountains figuring the Earth: five cardinal points, the highest of which, marking the centre, we know to be the pivot of the other four, the ones familiar to us. This earth onto which "He" steps emerges yet again—or eternally—from a kind of sea-womb of the seethings of an unstabilized creation, itself resting on still celestial clouds.

The end of an imperial progress forbidden today to all and sundry. But can we imagine a new Son of Heaven flying above all this? The signboards are categorical: no passage allowed.

Peking, Forbidden City: Terrace of the Hall of Gathering Essence (Zhongcui bao). Axial mountain and its satellites on base supporting a bronze crane.

Axis-of-the-world stones

Of the five mountains, the central one, the highest, marked the point from which the Emperors took off and to which they returned among mortals once more from their ritual journeys. At other times the "Sons of Heaven," sitting on their south-facing thrones, quenched their thirst with the forces of Yang and became identified with the Great Bear in an all-powerful immobility. Rites were thus performed from the thirteenth century onward inside the walls of the Forbidden City. Some traces remain of previous imperial capitals, but it is not necessary to immerse oneself in archaeological excavations to imagine an identical ritual in an identical architectural setting designed to reproduce the ideal space in which, according to Chinese cosmology, Emperor and Mountain are bound together.

33

Peking, Forbidden City: Courtyard on the north-east side.

Suzhou: Western Garden (Xiyuan) of the Hanshan Temple.

Peking, Forbidden City: Stone on base in the Garden of the Palace of Tranquil Longevity.

Before going into the question of the mountain, of the five or nine mountains, we shall make a detour by way of writing and cite the words of Kyril Ryjik in his historical prologue (p. 15) to *The Chinese Idiot*: "Thus the first written forms of what was to become Chinese script appeared on divinatory bones. Because these consisted of tiny marks scratched on bones, whereas elsewhere, on the walls of the Altamira or Lascaux caves, there are large painted figures, we have got into the habit of speaking of the first as writing and the second as painting. That is a piece of stupidity. Both are ritual narratives of events."

The modern written representation 山 of the concept of mountains derives from the pictogram ᨬ which portrayed three peaks, the one in the middle being higher than the others. The usual explanation is that since "three" engenders the plural, this sign represents a mountain chain. To this lucid explanation we should like to add that writing provided a fixed form for pre-existent thoughts, among them the idea that the mountain not only belonged to the earth but marked that earth as primeval.

At the centre of an earth which the ancients conceived of as square, there arose the axis-of-the-world mountain, plus four more mountains which,

placed at the cardinal points of the compass, stood at the limits of the earth. The earth in its essence was Yin, whereas the mountains held up the Yang essence in the circular and ever-moving sky. Later an attempt was made to locate or give material form to this earth-axis by identifying it with the Kunlun Mountains (fairly close to Tibet), on the strength of Vedic texts which spoke of the mythical Mount Meru as the invisible polar mountain on which the celestial worlds rose in tiers. Although this identification was only a passing fad, it proves nonetheless the interest taken in mountains down through the ages.

The Chinese preserve the memory of the old pictogram, permitting them to interpret instantly as axis-of-the-world stones isolated rocks or compositions of three, five or nine stones set on plinths in the Forbidden City or the gardens of the Summer Palace.

To understand the interest taken in stones in nature, to the point of placing them on display in the same way as works of art, it must be remembered that, quarried from mountains, torn from the beds of torrents or dredged up from the bottoms of lakes, they retain the marks of telluric energies in their textures, and that through them there circulates the Breath Force. Unshaped, uncarved,

35

they remain androgynous, and thereby express Creation in its pure state. To say that the Chinese do not carve stones, however, is inaccurate; for they use them in the decorative motifs of architectural groupings. But they know, or at least knew, that beneath the chisel of the craftsman-sculptor the vital principles are disjoined. The respect of the Chinese, and after them the Japanese, for stone as matter, led them to make rather sparing use of it in statuary.

Representations of the axis-of-the-world are very common, since the Emperors liked to surround themselves with emblems of power. These rocks, extremely phallic in aspect, have a relatively circular base, set on a stone plinth (most commonly square-shaped, but there are exceptions which do not lead us to generalize) ornamented with stereotyped designs. Towards the base of the plinth are cloud patterns supporting those of a sea which, in its frozen swirlings, seems molten; the upper part shows a sky swollen with clouds peopled by dragons, themselves flown over by a line of cranes with outspread wings. This plinth appears to us as an image of the beginnings of the earth. Yet at the same time, the combination of plinth and axial stone evokes for us the Hindu *lingam* standing erect on the square plane of its *yoni*, which, in India, bears several symbolic interpretations: that of Shiva, of the rising sun, of the union of the sun and the earth, of the cosmic egg and of Mount Meru; in other words, the symbols of Creation.

In an imposing display on the avenue bordering the lake of the Summer Palace gardens, the stones on plinths that have escaped depredations remain to manifest signs of powers: magic signs. They are One, for "One," said Laozi, "is the origin of the innumerable and the pivot of created beings... Just as Tao engenders One, so One engenders Two; Two engenders Three; Three engenders the infinity of creations."

Peking, Summer Palace: Two views of the same axis-of-the-world stone.

Above: Angular and abrupt side expressing the Yang forces.

Below: Side with soft and riddled shapes expressing the Yin forces.

▷ Peking, Forbidden City: Imperial Garden.

Fantastic stones

The infinity of creations: what would an Emperor have possessed who did not possess that?

The chronicles tell us that the craze for fantastic stones reached its height in the Tang period. At that time the market value of such stones exceeded that of the most celebrated paintings. In the eleventh century the senior scholar-official Su Shi had paid one hundred pieces of gold for a miniature stone known as Nine Peaks. In the twelfth century —three centuries, in other words, after the Tang dynasty—the Jürchen invaders were to destroy the extraordinary collections of the Emperor Huizong: collections of paintings, calligraphies, ancient coins, pieces of jade and objects from arch-

Peking, Forbidden City: Imperial Garden.

Peking, Forbidden City: Stones on base in the courtyard of the Palace of Inheriting Heaven (Xuanqiong).

aeological excavations carried out on sites dating from the second millennium B.C. In addition, the Emperor possessed a fabulous collection of curious stones. His minister, Zhu Mian, a native of Suzhou, who was himself interested in the wonderful eroded rocks of Lake Tai, had a monumental boulder forty feet high transported 400 miles to Kaifeng, then the capital of the Empire. The official history of the Songs, reporting the fact, mentioned that a warship and several thousand workers had been employed in that transport, which, besides, caused widespread damage to bridges and canal locks as well as to the ramparts of cities along the way. The imperial craze for stones—Huizong had the Empire ransacked for them, and some were destined to adorn a magic mountain built north-east of his palace—eventually led the country to its ruin. Huizong himself, dispossessed by invaders, ended his days unhappily in exile.

This attachment of the Sons of Heaven, and doubtless of all the aristocratic classes, to the odd stones they collected has its origin in the remotest historical times. For thousands of years the Chinese viewed the sky as the inside of an immense cave, detached fragments of which had formed the mountains. This archaic belief subsists in the pictogram for stone (shi) 石, which represented a stone breaking off from the inner wall of a cave: a memory that lingers throughout the mythical epochs of the Creation of the Universe and may still be discerned in the present written form 石. But the stone that dropped from the sky or the cave-vault was never regarded as an inert mass: during its fall the atmosphere revived it; breathed Qi into it; reenergized it.

Although the axis-of-the world stones do not really belong to the category of odd, exceptional stones which delighted the keen imperial collectors, they may be included in that category for the reason that they were deliberately singled out, selected to be mounted on pedestals, isolated from a "stone composition" context such as we shall encounter in the garden of the scholar. The exceptional minerals in the imperial catalogues that we are able to admire today are, apart from very rare and perfect stones from Lake Tai, chiefly crystals barely free of their coating of marine and subterranean concretions, and meteorites. And all of them, effectively exhibiting in their origins and textures the magical and beneficial forces, the combined virtues of Yin and Yang, are like so many manifestations of the infinite variety of creation.

Peking, Forbidden City: Stalagmite in the Imperial Garden.

Stalagmites and stalactites illustrating the supernatural aspect of mountain interiors always had a fascination for the Chinese. Aesthetically, they are said to act as a counterpoint to the contorted shapes of Taihu stones.

39

Peking, Forbidden City: Imperial Garden.
Sea-slug fossils and corals.

Peking, Zhongshan Park (Sun Yat-sen Memorial): Limestone block as carved by erosion.

Among the many varieties of stones, the most sought after come from the region of Lake Tai (Taihu); they are known accordingly as "Taihu stones." Found in limestone deposits acted upon in various ways by corrosive acids when in the Primary period, some 300 million years ago, the Yangzi delta was covered by the sea, they bear in their pitted surfaces and strange shapes the whole history of the Earth.
The great connoisseurs ranked them at the top of the hierarchy.
In the eighth century A.D. Bai Juyi wrote a long poem on them. In the twelfth century, in his catalogue of stones *The Cloud Forest*, Du Wan describes them as follows: "Taihu stones are produced by the waters of the Great Lake. They are hard and shiny, with strange reliefs like empty eye-sockets and twisted peaks. Some are white, others bluish black or a luminous blue. Their shapes form interwoven patterns; their surface is covered with small cavities hollowed out by wind and water. When struck, they ring with limpid clarity. Divers go after them with a chisel or mallet in their hand; it is hard work, collecting and choosing them. When a fine specimen is loosed in the water, stout ropes are slung around it, then it is hoisted on board the boat with a hand-winch. Stones whose shape lacks character may be worked with the chisel. Then they are aged by a fresh immersion, and so they may undergo unharmed the action of wind and rain and preserve their appearance unchanged."

Peking, Summer Palace: Taihu stone
on the north shore of Lake Kunming.

EMPEROR AND DRAGONS

Anonymous, Qing Dynasty:
The Emperor Kangxi in Ceremonial Dress. Painting on silk.

The dance of the dragons

Make-up Box, reign of Qianlong (1736-1795). Cloisonné enamel.

To reveal esoteric teachings of Tao bearing on the cosmic entity of China, the circulation of energies and the Breath Force, imagery had recourse to a mythological figure familiar from the dawn of antiquity: the dragon. In this form 𠃊𠃊 it was present in inscriptions on divinatory bones, then on ritual bronzes, beginning in the second millennium B.C. Between the first millennium and the second century B.C. wings were added to it.

Among its innumerable iconographic representations we have chosen this enamelled terracotta panel for the infinitely small land formed by three rocks at the bottom of the composition, a land that seems caught, gripped and supported by the strong claws of a pair of dragons. On a background of Cosmic Ocean, the colour of which, between blue and green, designates as being of Yin essence, two yellow dragons—Yang energy in its pure state—execute a cosmic dance which the physicist Kenneth Ford, speaking of protons in his *World of Elementary Particles*, calls "the dance of creation and destruction," recalling that all matter on earth or in space takes part in a continuous cosmic dance. And on this panel we see two symmetrical elements of the same size, the dragons, expressing the same energy, except that in one case it is positive and in the other negative. At the centre of rotation, the axis of symmetry, the energy of the Breath Force spurts out in the shape of an incandescent sphere. That energy is propagated through the cosmos like the radiation of electrical discharges, setting up vertical waves from the emergence of the Earth in the triple form of a vibrating mountain animated by whirling motions, fully charged with the energy just released.

By means of this theme, a thousand times repeated, Taoist mythology expounded from earliest times the theory of the primordial Big Bang which our contemporary laws of physics are now beginning to formulate.

Very early in their histories, the peoples of the plains and plateaus must have identified the formidable complex of towering mountains that form an arc from the Hindu Kush to the Indochina peninsula—the Himalayan folds—with the backbone of that fabulous creature which shook the earth with frequent tremors. But dragons, too, were the untamed and mighty rivers that flowed down from the heights of the West. Whoever sets eyes on them for the first time cannot help seeing in their ripples and eddies, in their capricious windings, the scales of a dragon.

The Far East is peopled with dragons, and wonderingly we endeavour to follow up their tracks and get our hands on them and puzzle out what they mean.

But dragon meanings, on that far side of the world, are not so readily ascertained. Coiled up in eccentric clouds or merging with symmetrical waves, they come forth unexpectedly, at one swoop, open-jawed, with darting tongue and wind-blown mane—come forth to sow the earth with their seed and vanish again, before we have had time to label them.

What we do know is that they help us or force us to measure the baffling distance that divides us from their ambiguous existence.

As far as our gaze can carry, it discovers them cast in bronze, angular and scaly, or embodied in the huge mask of the t'ao-t'ie, the primordial glutton figured by their confronted shapes.

Then in stone and clay they appear in successive bounds, unpredictable and astonishing, they too astonished perhaps to find themselves crawling over a mirror surface, shouldering a ritual jade or circling a vase which they cling to with their tapering tails or hold in their lustrous coils.

Intent on finding out their true nature, we question them and, learned and naïve, we think we have unlocked their secret when we put them down as springing from the alligator, the serpent or the lizard.

They grin and glide away along a sword blade, behind a medicine box, around an unmysterious bowl. We pursue them unafraid, knowing that they do not expect to be transfixed with a spear and driven to spit flames, like the fabulous and malefic monsters of the West, for they are honoured and singled out by this East which they fecundate by bringing down its spring rains, before making their way back into the deepening abysses of autumn.

Then we meet them again at the turn of a syllogism, in the pages of a book and the dust of a library, and we tie them down with triple cords in a variable enumeration: they are the Tao, they are Yang and the East, they are wood and greenness and the seasonal feasts. But imperturbable and improbable they have already set to playing with the sacred pearl, to chasing each other among the numberless reflections of sky and water, to coiling and interlacing and unlacing, and so to fade away into the transparency of glass and crystal.

Immutable dragons who cleave the timeless billows with the rapidity of legends, you have fallen into the grip of cunning morphologists who examine you under their magnifying glasses. And what do they find? Camel head, stag horns,

45

Peking, Summer Palace: Bas-relief on a wall of the east entrance.

cow ears, serpent neck, frog belly, hawk claws, says one. Tiger jaws, serpent body, alligator tail, lizard paws, says another.

Still others recite your claims: solemn and five-clawed, you are the emperor; yellow, you brought men writing; at Buddha's beck and call, you carry the aged saints on your back; coupling with a sow, you engender the elephant. And so on to the wits' end of psychologists, sociologists, demonologists.

Brought to a pause by so much zoological and mythological scrutiny, they roll their eyes like gleaming marbles, then taking advantage of a moment's inattention they are off again, their goatee unfurled, into the mazes of a reverie where the poet awaits them, the poet who will tame them.

For in the end you cannot really know a dragon until you invite him to come and live with you.

P.F. Schneeberger

Peking, Forbidden City: One of two enamelled terracotta panels
on either side of the gate of the Hall of Spiritual Cultivation (Yangxin dian).

Dragon shapes on the land mass of China

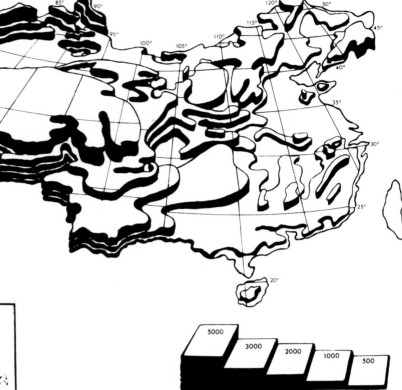

Plate from Wang Gai's *Mustard Seed Garden Manual of Painting*, illustrating a classical theme, 1679.

A painter drawing a dragon was blamed for putting no pupils in the eyes, but when he added them the dragon immediately flew away.

Schematic model of the general relief.

On the first map are to be seen the terracings of relief stretching in a physical descent from the high mountains of Central Asia stage by stage to the coasts, where the level of the land approaches zero altitude.

On the second map of China, with each dot representing 5,000 inhabitants, are the present population zones comprising according to recent censuses about a billion people, whereas in 1834 the population amounted to 400 million and by the first census in history, in the year 2 A.D., it totalled 57 million (slightly higher than the estimate given by J. Gernet in *Le Monde Chinois* for the Roman Empire in the same period). But it is clear that, apart from certain areas such as Heilongjiang, the places of human settlement, making all due allowances, have not changed: they correspond far more to the irrigated plains and plateaus than to the coastal regions.

48

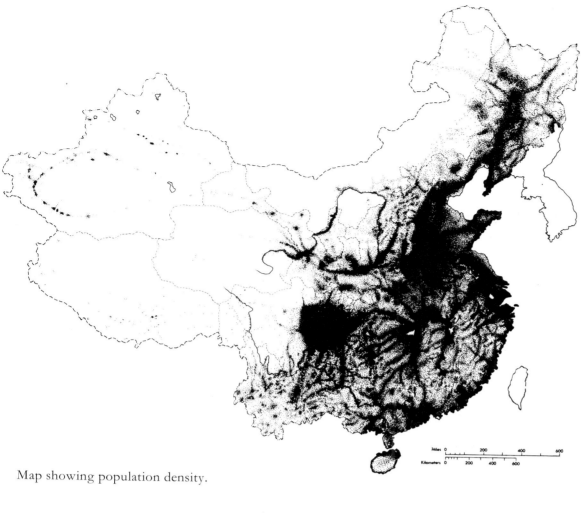

Map showing population density.

How to draw the imperial dragon motif. Illustration from an article by Yin Yuanzhen of the costume workshop of the Peking Opera.

Now that you have before you these dual maps of the same area, if you let your gaze travel over the enamelled terracotta panel of the dance of the two dragons, you will be able to make out in the undulations of the one on the left the relief contour of the mountains, while on the right-hand dragon is imprinted the population distribution, closely linked, in most cases, to the mountain network. Superimposed, these two maps, taken from different works, will reproduce exactly the cosmic dance of the dragons or the double rendering of a single dragon's track through space.

Celestial, subterranean, terrestrial, aquatic all at the same time, in its veins flows black and yellow blood:

Black like the sky
and yellow like the earth of China,

according to the *Book of Changes*.

The dragon cycle

Peking, Forbidden City:
Terrace of the Hall of Gathering Essence.
One of the two five-clawed dragons
(dragons at the top of the hierarchy).

In its path from the West to the Eastern seas the dragon has its original solid and male appearance, its Yang aspect, attenuated in favour of an aquatic predominance of Yin essence; in other words, as the level of the mountains drops, the rivers gorged with yellow blood broaden out and irrigate the plains. On reaching the sea the dragon once more takes off in flight; it is Leaping Dragon. When it has filled its body with ever-renewed clouds it is Flying Dragon; redescending toward its lair in the form of rain it becomes Soaring Dragon. After a period of repose it continues its endless cycle as

Hiding Dragon, underground, then as Field Dragon in the slight outcroppings of telluric energies on the surface of the soil; it reappears to humans as Visible Dragon in the courses of streams and rivers. Sixth in order, Visible Dragon is *qian*, the first of the sixty-four hexagrams, wholly Yang, of the *Book of Changes*. It expresses the force, the basic dynamism, of change regarded as an attribute of the sky.

Present in the temporal cycle of the seasons, the dragon makes his appearance in the spring: East and Spring are in correspondence; the dragon is then green, the green of the first shoots. At the spring equinox he flies off to become a celestial power and display himself in lightning when he has reached the highest point of his Yang intensity. At the autumn equinox, coloured an ochreous red, he once again comes down to earth.

As a celestial, creative, ordering power, the dragon cannot fail to be associated with the Emperor, the keeper of the calendar whose function is to guarantee the prosperity of the Empire by ensuring that order on earth is in conformity with celestial order. Sealed in walls, carved on steles, moulded in bronze, woven in the brocades of dignitaries' robes, dragons peopled and still people the palaces and imperial residences: dragon, a celestial power sprung from the waves. The pearl he holds between his raised claws may also symbolize the perfection and the orders of the Emperor: the indisputable splendour of his word of command.

△ Porcelain vase with red-copper underpainting, from the reign of Kangxi (1662-1722).

Suzhou: The Twin Pagodas (Shangta si). Stele of the cloud dragon.

51

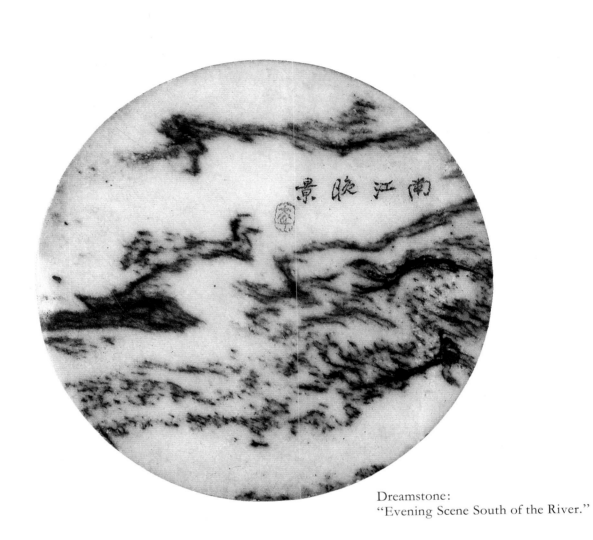

Dreamstone:
"Evening Scene South of the River."

MEDITATIVE INTERLUDE IN FRONT OF A DREAMSTONE

Race and dance of dragons;
expression of the structure of matter;
expression of the movements of the air;
expression of the folding of the mountains;
expression of the course of rivers.
Race and dance of the life principle
in its many and changing displays.
There was no need to be surprised
that the petrified veins
of a polished piece of the Tian Shan mountains
should be its witness.

Facing the indelible traces
of the swirl of energies
to which a man carving *Evening Scene South of the River*
and who signed with his artist's name of Da Jian
would give direction,
we are aware of nothing more than a state of soul
floating between time and space; nothing
but an expression of Tao.

MAN AND DRAGONS

To tame him, the archer Yi shoots at Hebo, lord of the Yellow River.
Plate from the *Chuci*, published under the Qing, 1645.

The descent of
the dragon

"The Ancients confided their inner transports of feeling to ink and paint brush by taking the route of landscape. Without transforming anything they adapted themselves to all transformations; without acting, they acted; living obscurely they attained glory; because they had put the last touches to their training and mastered life by setting down everything to be found in the Universe, they became infused with the very substance of mountains and rivers" (Shitao).[1]

We shall quote from, rather than paraphrase, the comments of Pierre Ryckmans on Shitao's *Remarks* concerning the opening of this eighteenth chapter:

"Painting is not a *transfer*, a plagiarism of the world, but a *reality* parallel to the world. The various concrete characters presenting respectively mountain and water are the implementation of abstract principles with which they have been endowed by Heaven (or Nature). The painter cannot be content with reproducing their concrete manifestations; he must journey within himself to their source, in other words, to those various principles themselves, with which, by the grace of Heaven, he too is infused. Thus it is not from the mountain or from water that he will take those various principles, since Heaven has granted them to him directly... This gift assumed by the painter has been conferred upon him by Heaven, and Heaven has endowed the mountain and water in the same way; the autonomous development of painting, far from being carried out in a vacuum, is thus achieved and takes its place in symmetry alongside other natural outward forms of Creation, inspired by a single ordering principle."

Mountain and water, 山 and 水, *shanshui*: two opposed signs united to give landscape painting its name.

In the ascending movements of the mountains and the plunging of the water, which seems to take an opposite direction, in the structure of the landscape thus formed, the vital forces, the breaths of creation, bring the space to life. In the first phase all is contradiction: the summit of the mountain seems in its puckerings irresistibly drawn to the sky, but the forest that clothes it joins the lower part of the

composition in its downward windings. From the mountaintop the water gushes in a violent cascade, but soon the torrent is masked by a scarf of vapours, which the sky seems to breathe in. From the empty patches of white mists and the filled-in areas of dark vegetation there is born movement: the cosmic dance ever portrayed.

On closer inspection, we may reveal the ornamental patterns of the structure by dividing the painting into three horizontal levels.

In the lower part of the upper third a waterfall gushes from the rocks. Its characteristic pattern was taken up and used by the Japanese stone raisers to express one type of garden waterfall. The various elements making up this top register of the landscape are simple: on the left the waterfall, in the centre the sharp drop of the mountain slope, on the right a secret upper glen concealed by clouds.

The Yin and Yang forces, which in the upper register are presented in a relation of quiet equilibrium, pervade the middle level with their vibrant pulsations. Here the course of the high waterfall is soon masked by ever denser vapours clinging to the rockface. A white body, the Soaring Dragon, occupies the centre of this middle register. Tucked between the vaporous meanders are two huts, one fairly well visible, the other concealed at the base of the clouds trailing from the upper level.

On the left side, at the bottom of the middle register, is a small figure, the man with a staff, who has just entered the composition.

While the two upper levels develop the parallel course of the dragon, the lower one consecrates their reunification in the interlacings of trees, rocks, stumps and torrents, in which—as in the fascinating and disturbing "composite heads" of Arcimboldo—one may make out the forefeet and maw of the dragon, now single again. In the cavern of its jaws the painter has placed two townsmen in a thatched pavilion perched on poles, a "folly" for wise scholars, a familiar spot in the Gardens of Longevity. Despite the traces of a path, the two men have probably reached this junction of the Breath Forces by means of the moored boat, steered by a servant concealed in the shrubbery between the dragon's paws.

Kun Can (1612–c. 1692), Qing Dynasty: High Mountains and Long Streams, view of Tiandu Peak in the Huangshan Mountains (Anhui). Paper scroll.

Because of the solitary figure it contains, we should like to interpret the second painting as the continuation of the mental journey of the two figures in the preceding one. The mountain never comes to an end; as soon as the last foothills are left behind we hope to reach the summit, but in that instant we discover other folds, other heights that were hidden from our view by the first. Thus this physical ascent which is the material form of the spiritual ascent remains an unending pursuit.

Was that little man with a staff climbing towards his lofty retreats a woodcutter or a hermit? And did the two scholars, between two glasses of wine, recite the poem of Jia Dao (779-843)?

The pillow at the bed-head is a stone from the stream;
From the well the spring descends through bamboos to
[*the pool.*
After midnight the guest was not yet asleep,
Listening alone to the rain coming from the mountains.

Comparing the vegetation covering the cliffs of the summits in the previous painting and in this one, we see that the less wooded mountain here is undoubtedly higher: without realizing it we have gone on to the portrayal of a landscape at higher altitude. In this composition we must also note the rendering of the distant mountain: in the background loom inaccessible peaks (1). This vision of the "distant mountain" will be expressed, as we shall see, in the Gardens of Longevity.

On the shelf, below the "near summit" of the upper left-hand part, where the first manifestations of energy are concentrated in the waters of the run-off, we observe a small basin (2), an almost closed form with the hint of a peninsula, the evocation of Soaring Dragon (p. 53), like a prototype of the garden ponds in China and later in Japan.

From the collecting pool, through a narrow cleft, a waterfall (3) escapes in a vertiginous drop. An initial block of stone, fallen from the summits, obstructs its course (4), varies its fall and diminishes its force, creating a second waterfall in the widened gap spanned by a footbridge (5). In the foamings of the third cascade the water, in stages (6), gradually loses its force, striking the obstacles in its path at no more than very slow speed: once again it becomes the bearer of the energies of the Breath Force, in the same way as the receiving basin of the upper shelf. At the end of this tumultuous course the painter has placed a figure who seems to be drinking in the beneficent emanations. At the meeting point of

land and water (7), he stands in the dragon's maw: a dragon which in this composition is presented in its entirety. Vertically above the figure, between the branches of the trees, we make out a vaguely defined circular or spherical mass, without being able to say whether it represents the eye or the lair of the dragon (8).

At the foot of the mists from which rise the distant mountains we come upon the roofs of a hermit's hut with two storeys (9), perhaps a Buddhist monastery. Its location in just this spot, as we shall later see, is by no means the work of chance; no whim of the artist's.

Following the progress of the paths, which our eye loses and finds again, we become aware of the high art in the depiction of different planes; of the depth of field that is far more in evidence here than in the previous composition. Leading from the hermit's hut—a knoll hides its start (10)—we see the path reappear in the open space of a shelf (11); then it is once more blocked from view by the steep pale-tinted mountain, behind which we guess it forks; on one hand it continues to climb towards the head of the waterfall, but it also joins the footbridge thrown over the mountain stream (12).

Like the previous painting, this one is in its entirety an evocation of the descent of the dragon through the medium of the mountain in all its furrows, all the vegetation which covers it. Very early in the history of landscape painting, the painters took as part of their task to give expression to the arteries or pulse of the dragon; that is, to the inner energy currents which Chinese geomancy attributes to mountains ("This idea plays an essential role in the conception of the composition, giving it unity and organic dynamism" [2]), and the painter who neglected those currents would simply restrict himself to the outward manifestation of forms.

Water dragon in the first landscape, through vapours of mist and smoke that, in the structural dialectic of *shanshui*, take on the role of water and, in plastic terms, make it possible to combine filled and empty spaces. Mountain dragon in the second landscape; the dragon we have so often encountered sculpted in low reliefs, in paintings, in the most concrete realism as in the most subtle suggestions, is here totally integrated, never absent. He winds his way—they wind their ways, twinned or manifold: soaring aloft in wreaths of incense from a perfume burner or, just as easily, in heaviness of bronze, where, presented withdrawn into himself, he becomes unrivalled in his cosmic course.

Shen Zhou (1427-1509), Ming Dynasty:
Lofty Mount Lu,
painted in 1467 for his master's 70th birthday.
Paper scroll.

Wang Hui (1632-1717), Qing Dynasty:
Water and Marsh Landscape in the style of Zhao Danian.

The dragon drivers

The first two landscape paintings presented here, which will not be the last, have shown us figures infinitely small but never swallowed up in imposing spaces; quite the contrary, they were always portrayed either at the meeting point of beneficent emanations or about to go there.

The presence of figures in landscape paintings may be understood on three levels.

On the aesthetic, compositional level they appear as references, giving the sites a size-scale; they are a reminder of the identification of painting with poetry and of poetry with painting; an identification that is the hallmark of artistic creation in China. The painters were in the habit of quoting poems especially suited to induce inspiration. Shitao wrote: "To extract a painting from a poem is a matter of instinct and temperament, not of borrowing a painting from such and such a painter and making a poem about it afterwards. Extracting a poem from a painting springs naturally, in the moment of inspiration, from the same mental universe. It is not a case of arbitrarily absorbing a poem, dissecting it and making a painting out of it afterwards. For the person who truly grasps their mutual relations, the exchange is like that of a mirror which reproduces an image without the existence, at the outset, of the slightest preconceived intention. But people today inevitably fall into an arbitrary conception of these relations between poetry and painting." [3]

Philosophically, the figures in the landscape testify to the place of man in the Universe, to his participation in the Universal Order. He is neither master nor guest of a world created once and for all in the splendour of its perfection. The Creation, of which he is an integral part, remains incomplete, and man must dedicate his life to perfecting the Earth.

In short, we attribute to these figures a didactic role. The position chosen for them by the artists in their landscapes is never without significance. The figures, by their position, mark out the most beneficent places in nature for man.

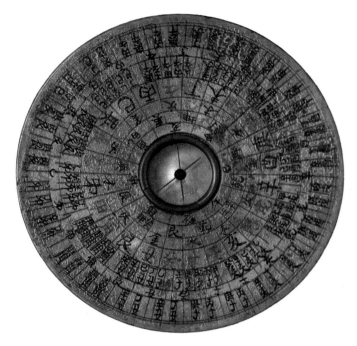

Geomancer's compass (*luopan*) of varnished wood with eight reading rings. Contemporary work.

A compass of this type was copied by the Jesuit Henry Doré for his book Recherches sur les superstitions en Chine, *published between 1911 and 1938. Few Chinese compasses are so simplified; they usually have from 16 to 20 rings out of the 38 prescribed in the treatises. If we number the rings starting from the centre, the first contains the magnetic needle, and the second, divided into 16 pigeon-holes, has the 8 cardinal points written in archaic ideograms. The next rings are divided into multiples of 12 (24, 72 and 120). In the third figure the names of the 12 trigrams. In the fourth, the triple repetition of 4 of the 5 Elements: Wood, Fire, Metal, Water (the Element Earth being omitted). This type of compass indicates the direction of the* Breath Forces *connected with the cardinal points. From it can be determined the corrections in topography needed to counter baneful currents.*

Tradition tells us that the great Yu, successor of the five mythical rulers, tamed with the help of dragons the overabundant waters of the terrible rivers that brought prosperity to the country but also, in their periodic floods, sowed destruction. Marking out and digging their beds, keeping their wildness within bounds, he laid out the structure of the territory. By the second millennium B.C. everything seemed to have been put in place, and sedentary farmers settled at the foot of their dragon mountains, in the windings of their dragon rivers. The great Yu may be considered the precursor of the unbroken line of specialists in the problems of organizing space, known as the Fengshui Masters,

or Masters of Wind and Water, also called the Dragon Drivers. In the Han period investigation into magnetic fields led to the invention of a device, the ancestor of the compass, in which a magnetized piece of metal indicates the North-South axis. It was used to point out the South, the Emperor having to face in that direction, the order of the earth being an exact copy of that of Heaven.

In their inquiries into places having the maximum concentration of energies, in other words into places steeped in the Breath Force, the Fengshui Masters discovered that these were usually situated above underground springs.

Among the tasks of the Fengshui specialists was that of detecting those concentrations of energies, for the greatest benefit of mankind; of tapping those positive energy currents that come down from the mountains and leading them toward the plains, toward inhabited areas; and, also, of warding off the negative currents. When the natural site of human settlement did not correspond exactly with the geomantic data, gigantic operations were then undertaken to restructure the terrain. As examples we may cite the changes made to river courses, the filling-in of mountain ridges in some cases to block the passage of winds carrying noxious breaths, and the raising of artificial hills such as Coal Hill (Meishan) north of the Forbidden City.

According to Taoist ethics, manipulations of the earth's surface alter the internal current of the Breath Forces; that is why it is important to avoid "waking the dragon," in other words, wounding him in his vital parts by clumsy interventions and arousing his wrath. On the scale of the Chinese land mass, manipulations of landscapes, supervised by geomancers, were done carefully, with respect for their irregularities and with the preservation of their organic aspect. These preoccupations remained constant for more than two millennia.

Today, and virtually at international level, the attention of governmental bodies (often, indeed, preceded by a marginal vanguard which revealed man's dilapidation of nature on a planetary level for quick profits) is turning increasingly to the study of ecosystems, over which Chinese geomancers had kept watch since earliest times.

The field of action of the Fengshui Masters extended from the founding of urban sites and the establishment of villages or simple dwellings to the selection of sites for tombs and drilling wells. Geomancers are still officially consulted in Hong Kong and Taiwan on all area planning.

The dragon's lair

In nearly all parts of the country, the Chinese even today prefer and insist on a house facing south. "One may wonder why this orientation is so generally adopted, in latitudes as far apart as those of Peking, Shanghai and Canton, both in town and in villages, both in temporary homes or shelters and in solidly built houses. The explanation lies in the exposure to sun. Despite climatic differences from one region to another, the common concern is to receive the maximum amount of sunshine in winter and to be protected from it in summer. Now direct southern exposure makes this result possible, especially in the continental climate of northern China. And the further south one travels, the higher the sun climbs in the sky and the less it enters the rooms in summer. So that the southward facing house remains desirable even in the southernmost regions." [4]

This deep-seated insistence on having a house facing south raises thorny problems for contemporary town planners and architects. Leon Hoa explains this desire in a rational way, but it is a desire in which we also see the vigorous ancestral tradition handed down by the Fengshui Masters, who systematically sited the house in accordance with the guiding principles of the Dragon's Lair.

Qiu Ying (c. 1510-1551), Ming Dynasty: Landscape in the style of Li Tang. Section of a silk scroll.

Siting of the Dragon's Lair according to a Fengshui manual. ▷

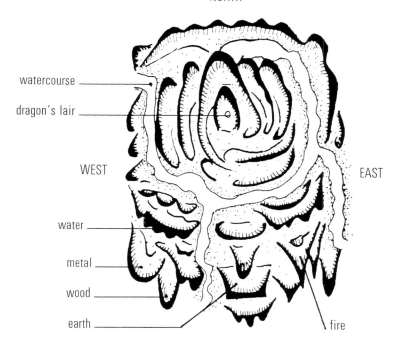

NORTH

watercourse

dragon's lair

WEST

EAST

water

metal

wood

earth

fire

Spring Travellers. Copy of the painting by Zhan Ziqian (551-604, or late 7th century) in the Old Palace Museum of Peking. The earliest known scroll representing a landscape or, more probably, a garden. Detail of a silk scroll.

棲霞總圖

Anonymous (18th century): Two plates from the album *Palaces of the*

Outside the cities, Buddhist monks always tried to site their monasteries in naturally sheltered places affording a maximum concentration of Breath Forces; *in each case the site corresponded to the* Dragon's Lair.
In the lefthand plate inscribed Qi xia zong tu *("General Plan of the Crimson Cloud Home"), the buildings face south and stand in a hollow at the foot of the mountains protecting them on the west, east and*

幽居巷

Emperor along the road from Peking to Suzhou, six or seven leagues from each other.

north. The site chosen is comparable in every way to that
of the prototypes reproduced on previous pages.
The righthand plate is inscribed Yu jü'an ("Small
Shrine of Solitary Retreat"). The buildings are huddled
at the foot of rock formations which channel and focus
the energies of the distant mountain visible to the north-
east. Not much work was needed for the monks to adapt
this natural garden to their requirements.

Didactic drawing from a 19th century book on garden design in ancient China.

alternating in the rhythmic expression of the mountain, while the sky, uniformly red-ochre, symbolizes the perfect Yang. The dragon that springs from the waters leaps upward to reascend toward the sky.

Originating in Central Asia, the crossroads of several great civilizations, this fresco fragment remains for us one of the most beautiful images of the expression of Tao in the way the symbolic colours found in all Taoist iconography have here been used to convey the balance and harmony of apparently antagonistic forces.

This piece of pottery, a small-scale model and precious memento of a vanished garden; this remnant of a wall painting removed from its context and set up in a museum, come from widely separated sites yet express an identical preoccupation: the importance of manipulations of the earth's surface according to the laws of geomancy to tap telluric forces in investigations that are probably as old as the origins of settled communities on the earth.

Of the older gardens we know nothing but what can be gleaned from paintings, novels and stories, and a few objects such as this glazed palette of the Tang period recently discovered in a tomb. It is a scaled-down landscape in which the arc of the mountains shelters a body of water. The mountains are puckered, undulating, animated to represent the Dragon's Veins in the alternation of upright Yang elements and the flowings and hollows of Yin essence. Near the water three mushrooms are growing: they symbolize the magic mushrooms, the ingestion of which, according to Taoist tradition, gave admission to immortality.

For a parallel reading we have a fragment of a wall painting dating from the ninth century, found at Bäzäklik, a Central Asian site along the Silk Road. Differing from some commentaries on this fragment, we cannot interpret the landscape as a clumsy representation, but as the realistic evocation of a landscape designed by man for an initiatory interpretation or as a reminder of the observance of rules for life. Whether the summits in the background are actual mountains or their symbolic rendering in the garden is of little importance in relation to the plantation of trees on the terraces laid out at the edge of the water, the matrix from which rises a dragon. From the blue-green, cold Yin tint rises the red-ochre male force, the warm Yang shade: the opposition of these tones is found

Ink palette found in a tomb at Zhongbao (Shaanxi). 8th century. Three-colour ware.

64

Bäzäklik (Turfan region, on the Silk Road): Wall painting
in Temple 19. 9th century.

The manipulation of sites

Permanent capital of the Empire since the fifteenth century, Peking stands to the south-west of a small plain in the prolongation of the vast North China plain. This northern prolongation is bounded to the west and north-east by mountains rising little by little (1,300 to 1,650 feet, then 3,300 to 5,000 feet) in the direction of the Mongolian plateau. At an average altitude of 150 feet above sea level, the plain is formed partly by alluvial deposits the rivers have brought down from the mountains, chiefly the Yongding river which has its source on the Mongolian plateau and enters the plain from the west. This turbulent river has changed its course several times, altering the appearance of the plain each time and sometimes causing great damage. Within a radius of sixty miles to the west, south and east of Peking, archaeological sites testify to an intense culture as early as the Neolithic period, corresponding to the first dynasty of the traditional history of the Xia illustrated by Yu the Great. This succession of civilizations in a distinct area was not the result of chance and can be related to the theories concerning the choice of man's sites in privileged places, such as we find in all settled cultures. If then, by its setting of mountain ranges and the plentiful water of its rivers and springs, this region actually corresponded on a vast scale to geomantic requirements, it was nevertheless necessary, working on a less vast scale, to remodel these ideal conditions in accordance with the Fengshui precepts, when it came to building large residences.

The construction of the Forbidden City called for gigantic development works; and further works were undertaken to subdue and contain the Yongding river, which often broke the defences raised against it. Existing lakes were enlarged, and canals dug. Man-made hills were raised against the terrible north wind always sweeping this region. Among these works modifying and manipulating large sites are those of Beihai Lake, begun in the thirteenth century by Qubilai, along a north-south axis to the west of the present Forbidden City; the Meishan (Coal Hill) north of the palace, raised in the first half of the fifteenth century with earth taken from the ditches around the site of some hunting grounds; the immense complex of Yiheyuan (where "harmony is cultivated") commonly called the Summer Palace, some twelve miles north-west of Peking. This territory had first been set aside as game preserves. It was modelled by several princes, then emperors, who settled there to escape the torrid summers in the capital. The lakes, at first quite small, were considerably enlarged; here again, the earth removed was used to heighten the existing hills. Throughout historical times, this site was manipulated on a vast scale. The changes made showed the concern of their designers for drainage and improvement, hence for better living conditions; they were *oriented* manipulations, directly related to the Fengshui rules.

The Emperor Qianlong was one of the last great organizers of development projects. Rounding off the work of his predecessors, he completed the artificial lakes and hills with architectural adjuncts inspired by the advice of Jesuit missionaries with whom he kept for some time on good terms, without however excluding other creeds. The Jesuit painters whom he welcomed to his court taught his artists European techniques of perspective. In their watercolours, these hack artists, without attaining flights of genius, nevertheless faithfully portrayed their subject, and recall for us the sometimes composite glories of the vast Summer Palace as the Emperor Qianlong transformed it.

Pages 67, 68, 70, 71:

Yuan Ming Yuan, Summer Palace near Peking and outskirts.
40 topographical views.
Four plates from two watercolour albums by
Tang Dai and Shen Yuan, 1744.

66

In the foreground, a hog-backed bridge over a water-course with the same bend as that of the Golden River canal in the Forbidden City. This is a wholly man-made site, except for the mountains visible to the north.

In the axis of the entrance, between the main palace and the artificial lake, a composition of raised stones evokes distant mountains and reconstitutes the sheltering horse-shoe amphitheatre.

67

In the search for lost gardens, this watercolour bids us wander round the less solemn grounds of a "farmhouse," rustic dependence of the Summer Palace.

Like the preceding site, this one is also remodelled on a composition very similar to that of the Qiu Ying picture (p. 60). We have again water, mountains, protecting trees. Here a well is placed in the Dragon's Lair, but wells and springs in China belong to the dragon of underground waters. From

the well, a wooden pipe takes water to irrigate a picturesque little rice field, which completes this rural fantasy.

From this watercolour, we have an engraving made during the same period by a Western artist who tried in his work to recreate the Chinese atmosphere. It is interesting to put the two works side by side. At first sight identical, on closer examination, they are seen to be different. We note that some details have been left out by the engraver, among them the typical placing of stone compositions alongside the water, probably a canal: "The canals are not aligned, the rustic stones bordering them are set with such great art that they seem to be the work of nature," wrote Brother Attiret, a Jesuit and painter at the court of the Emperor Qianlong, in his *Edifying Letters* (1743). The path leading to the upper pavilion surrounded by distant mountain compositions has also disappeared, whereas in the colour wash it is very evocative of progress towards the Dragon's Lair. By omitting or displacing trees, for example the cherry trees round the well, he has effaced some very important effects.

While the *descent of the dragon* can be clearly traced in the Chinese work, it has completely disappeared from the engraving. Owing to this absence of linkages, elements placed alongside each other have lost their meaning because the engraver (who wanted to be a faithful copyist) disregarded the symbols they expressed.

Documents of this kind were the models for the first Anglo-Chinese gardens in Europe, which were sometimes called "English gardens" to distinguish them from the geometrically laid out "French gardens." It is not surprising therefore that the traditional Fengshui rules were not applied, since only the formal aspect of the imperial gardens was conveyed and not the reasons for their design.

The painters of landscape like the model for the Tang garden (p. 64) and the Bäzäklik fresco (p. 65) show the continuous search through different epochs for the ideal site. It is not to be wondered at that the stone raisers, Masters of Gardens, should alike have followed the Fengshui development rules in laying out the microcosm of the Gardens of Longevity.

Plate from the *15th Notebook of Chinese Gardens. Gardens of the Emperor of China in 28 plates*, engraved by Le Rouge, 1786.

In China, the first place where we came on the Gardens of Longevity was on the north shore of Lake Beihai, during the visit to the Serenity Study (Jingxinzhai) built by the Emperor Qianlong. This is quite a simple garden, different altogether from the elaborate layout of the Summer Palace; it was intended to be a place of retreat and meditation, after the style of the scholars' gardens.

On the scheme of the garden in the folder handed out with the entrance ticket, the visitor finds the familiar image of the dragon, met with so often already in the most diverse guises, sometimes highly realistic, sometimes hinted at in the course of a river or the shape of a mountain. So, before entering the garden, he knows that he will meet it again, and already traces its head in the height to the west, topping an eight-sided pavilion; then, taking a leap as far as the two-storied pavilion in the north-west corner, the crowning point of the whole, he sees the covered gallery along which he can tread its

curved chine and follow it downwards to the half-moon marble bridge. He can also see on the plan, before losing himself in the maze of compositions in the garden, the strict south-north axial alignment of the main buildings and the different aspects of the two bridges spanning the second pond, the formal and stately classical marble one to the east, while the footbridge to the west, at the base of the dragon's head, tallies in its broken lines with the carefree spirit of the walk. As in the imperial residence described above (p. 67), an open pavilion forms the centre of the composition, on the axis of the ornamental ponds, at this focal point of all the energies of the Breath Forces channelled there by the rocks, representing the mountain. The plan highlights the double horseshoe of the protecting rocks, which surround the pavilion and site it at the place called the Dragon's Lair, in just the same way as in the picture illustrating the ideal site for human habitation (p. 60).

北 海 静 心 斋 平 面 示 意 图

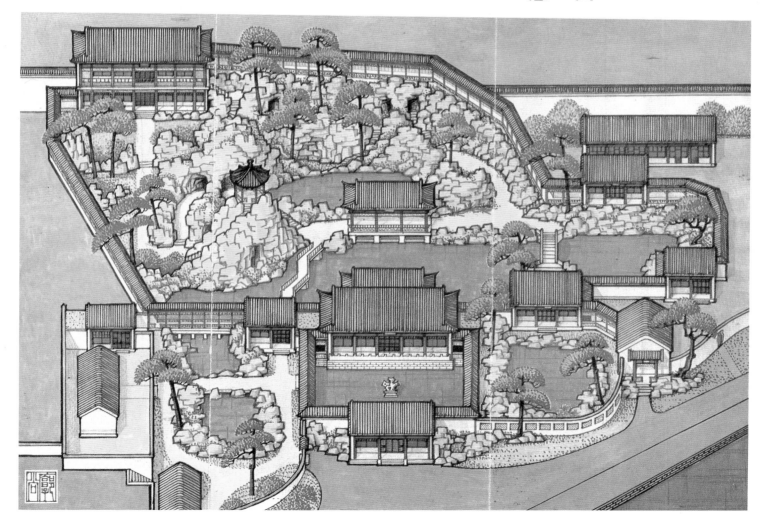

72

Peking, Beihai Park: Serenity Study Garden, laid out in 1757.
Looking north-west, with the central pavilion and belvedere.

◁ Peking, Beihai Park: Plan of the Serenity Study Garden (Jingxinzhai).

The mountain and its double

Anonymous, Song Dynasty: Countless Peaks and Valleys. Paper scroll.

"I have sought extraordinary peaks, I have made sketches of them, mountains and rivers have met in my mind and their imprint has been transformed there, so that finally they come back to me as Dadi," wrote Shitao. [5]

Guo Xi, a painter and theoretician who lived at the beginning of the eleventh century, recalled that the "artist must also, whether in carriage or on horseback, cover in his travels a good half of the Universe, and then only will he be able to take up the brush." [6]

Inspired artist or sensitive scholar, the stone raiser, familiar with the Chinese universe, liked to evoke famous sites and sites sung by poets. A stone dragon for a Garden of Longevity, a mountain by an unknown painter of the Song dynasty; we do not know whether the same landscape is portrayed, but we notice that the theme is the same, the summit of the mountain and its repetition in the form of a rock at the foot of it. In the painting, it overhangs a few buildings, it is the last trait of the mother-mountain, reproducing its silhouette along the edge of the plateau. In the composition of the Xiaopangu garden at Yangzhou (p. 77), it is the infant child, the last link in the cosmic dance. In both cases its role is to bring man nearer to the forces at the summit.

The identification of the stone with the mountain is a common theme in Chinese treatises for the use of painters (more than 800 of these are known today).

In one such treatise, an eighteenth century author holds forth at length on the different ways of drawing stones and concludes "to draw a mountain is the same thing." This was put by Shitao as follows: "Man can reconstruct a larger being in miniature without losing anything of it; once the mind has formed a clear image of it, the brush will go to the root of the matter." [7] That is to say, according to Pierre Ryckmans, "the idea is that painting is to the universe what the microcosm is to the macrocosm." [8]

A painter of genius, Shitao also created gardens at Yangzhou; vestiges of these remain and it is to be hoped that one day they will be restored. No longer working in brush and ink, but with materials borrowed from nature, the stone raisers, too, sought and expressed the identity between the

羽 披 雲 氣 裳 徒 襄
流 雲 無 指 點 小
澗 留 我 石 松 育 眠
白 鶴 夢 尔 步 登
雲 石 機
乾 隆 己 未 御 題

Lu Guang, Yuan Dynasty: Pavilions and Monasteries
in the Mountain of the Immortals, 1330s. Silk scroll.

infinitely great and the infinitely small, the structure of the universe and that of matter.

Crowned with a pavilion, in the Garden of Serenity Study (Jingxinzhai) the dragon uncurls, filling all the space; his ritualized descent near the habitation of man is not always as clearly shown, it can also be merely suggested by a single trait in which the Whole is embodied. Of the dragon that rises proudly in the Garden of the Small Winding Valley (Xiaopangu) at Yangzhou, like the dragon of the Bäzäklik fresco (p. 65), only the head and upper body seem to emerge from the waters—sea or river?—of the ornamental pool.

The eroded, holed rocks taken from Lake Tai have been composed, amalgamated, by the stone raiser to show the swirling force of the dragon; the stones were not cut but chosen for their texture, the pattern of their veins. And this dragon can be felt, surging, bounding, open mouthed, eyes bursting from their sockets; he bears on his back a six-sided pavilion. He leaps up, flies overhead, holds sway. His head rises above the level of the roofs; he drinks in the beneficent fragrance of space; the lines of his movement enfold a small pavilion level with the water, sited always at the same focal point.

He can be said to be outsize, gigantic, almost impossible to grasp, and indeed he would be, if there did not appear on his breast, beyond a footbridge he dominates, his exact portrait in miniature, made of a stone of a different texture—a stone from a mountain or torrent—child or double of himself which sheds over the passer-by walking along the striking composition the same flow of vital energy.

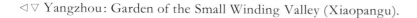

◁▽ Yangzhou: Garden of the Small Winding Valley (Xiaopangu).

陶泓三沐更
三薰袖手臨
流春臺雲倚
欲男山料長
片由末菓許
朱晉閣
壬午春日
御題

百道飛流下散瀉欲其野硯石在
笑墓花四伴漬烟根盤硯松陰畑
手肴
清流長潤潤白日亭全作一洗睨月
此流首山石詩乃先生所作于命書以
先童如
中宮長生運軒徙

Chen Luo, late Ming Dynasty:
The Washing of the Ink Stone. Paper scroll.

The scholar poet Mi Fu (1051-1107) is said to have been a most discriminating connoisseur of stones; his passion for them was carried to extravagance. When in 1105 he took up his appointment as magistrate in the Wu Wei district and entered the official precincts for the first time, his eye was caught at once by the magnificent rock adorning the garden. Forgetting all about protocol and etiquette, he greeted no one but bowed low before the stone and respectfully addressed it as "Shixiong," i.e. "Elder Brother Rock." Whether true or invented, the story was handed down and became a favourite theme with literati painters, who always took good care to harmonize the folds of his robe with the texture of the stone.

Communion between man and rock was a constant feature of Chinese painting. Identical, in the work by Chen Luo, are the silhouette of the small riverside figure and that of the cliff above him.

MAN AND STONES

Mi Fu's Homage to the Stone. Plate from Wang Gai's *Mustard Seed Garden Manual of Painting*, 1679.

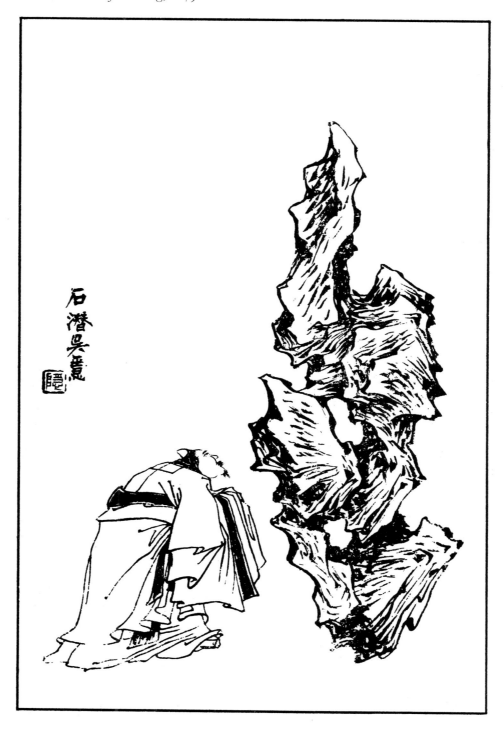

The scholar in his garden

Suzhou: Woodwork panel in the former residence of the king of the Taiping, now the Municipal Museum.

The scholar or literatus, in Chinese *wenren*, is literally the man (*ren*) of signs (*wen*). Originally the word *wen* meant vein, fracture, sign; it was close to the character *bu* (divinatory fissures). It later took on the meaning of literary composition, of culture, civilization; it also designated the civil power as opposed to *wu*, military power. In time of peace, in the pacified provinces, the administration was in the hands of the *wenren*.

The literati class of scholar civil servants arose in the fourth and third centuries B.C., when palace duties were no longer exercised hereditarily by the nobility. Under the Han dynasty, the social hierarchy was already very elaborate, and the power of the great landowning families was strengthened in an obvious attempt to thwart the ambitions of the new rising class of the great mer-chants who, regardless of their real economic pow-er, were still at the bottom of the social scale. From this time on, the scholar civil servant, at all levels and whatever his origins or fortune, was recruited for the administration through competitive exam-inations based on the "classical" Five Books, or one of them, according to the period. He was versed in philosophy, learned literature, music, poetry and, since he was a master of signs, in calli-graphy and painting. As far as his means allowed, he collected books and works of art.

The religious world of ancient China gave cur-rency to a number of basic notions which the si-nologist Marcel Granet calls the substance of Chi-nese thought. This body of knowledge had already taken shape at the time of the Zhou. The first Chi-nese philosophies drew on it for their inspiration; two or three centuries before the Christian era both the religion of Tao and the Confucian system took their main concepts from it, afterwards grafting on to them contributions from foreign religions, the influence of Buddhism being the most typical.

Convinced that the exercise of power by a hereditary aristocracy was doomed to failure, Confucius advocated the development of a moral authority grounded in "religious" values; the ruler, divinely appointed Son of Heaven, was in duty bound to align his conduct with the cosmic order, and if his management of affairs was clumsy, natural disorders could result. Confucius had been a visionary. After travelling the length and breadth of the land and meeting all its rulers in order to convince them of the soundness of his views (with-out much success), he took the road back to his native land, the kingdom of Lu, and devoted him-self to teaching. His doctrines were taken up and expanded by other philosophers including Mengzi, an idealist, and Xunzi. The latter rejected any kind of religious or irrational elements, holding that the social order was a necessary structure for life in common and the division of labour and, in agree-ment with Confucius, that order could not be main-tained by laws; the only way of governing was to shape morals by education. There was also the School of Legalists who deemed that society could not be governed by morals but only by a system of rewards and punishments, hoping the while that the latter would not have to be inflicted.

Tang Yin (1470-1524), Ming Dynasty: Tao Gu Composing ▷
a Lyric. Silk scroll.

一宿国槥遽旅中短訶聊以
識泥海當時我作陶歌吉
何必尊前面發紅唐寅

81

Suzhou: Lion Grove Garden (Shizilin).

From the second century B.C., the rulers were on the one hand eager to establish Confucian orthodoxy and, on the other, fired with enthusiasm for Taoist notions and techniques. Thus the moral authority and rational thought that were the basis of the establishment coexisted with the Taoist school, which at the same time preserved magical and religious practices already having little to do with the philosophical and mystical theories of the great masters such as Laozi and Zhuangzi, who deemed all political ambition and all concern with public affairs only vanity, and held out the prospect of union, through difficult ascetical discipline, with Tao, the principle of the universe.

The scholar, Confucianist by virtue of his function, carried out the duties of his social office; ancestor worship went hand in hand with the founding of a family and having children. At the same time, steeped as he was in Taoist doctrines tinged with Buddhism, he found his private pleasure in poetry and music. He was ever mindful of the Breath Forces and the means of permeating himself with them by sojourning in the most propitious places, near mountains and water. Unable to occupy the same post for more than three or four years, he was often on the move and took advantage of his travels to visit the most remarkable places in the empire. Poems and paintings bear witness, in the course of centuries, to the scholar's travels and aspirations. In his memoirs, *Six Stories as the Fickle Days Go By*, Shen Fu, a modest scholar of the late eighteenth century, tells of his life, dreams and travels, giving us a portrait of the Chinese scholar which seems to have changed little in the span of over a thousand years.

Whether living in a luxurious residence or a humble home, the scholar tried to reconstitute this vision of a universe liberated, in part, from social constraints, by arranging and patterning the space of his garden; in other words, by raising stones.

You Qiu (16th century), Ming Dynasty:
Elegant Gathering
in the Western Garden.
Paper scroll.

This meeting took place under the late Northern
Song in the residence of Wang Shen, the Emperor's
son-in-law. Li Gonglin was present and painted a
picture of it, now lost, which Mi Fei commented on.
By comparing You Qiu's picture with Mi Fei's text,
it is possible to identify the figures:
1. The Taoist Chen Bixu
2. Qin Shaoyou
3. Wang Shen
4. Su Dongpo writing a poem on a rock
5. Li Gonglin
6. Mi Fei
7. Wang Zhongzhi
8. Yuantong Dashi
9. Liu Juji
Mi Fei's text mentions sixteen participants.
You Qiu represented only eleven, but if he did
not keep literally to the text, he did keep to the
spirit of it.

Yuan Jiang, Qing Dynasty: Landscape in the Eastern Garden.
Detail of a silk scroll.

Closed spaces and distant views

Suzhou: Garden of the Master of the Fishing Nets (Wangshiyuan).

Closed spaces where distant views, landscapes visited in the past, poetic or pictorial memories, can be created anew, the gardens of scholars were situated in urban areas, on plains or low plateaux, rather than at the foot of high mountains. They were, therefore, a very intellectual representation of the idea of nature, of the "Mountains and Rivers," 山川, the first name given to landscape painting, before it was written "Mountain and Water," 山水.

Made by their owners in their image, the scholars' gardens mirrored their contradictory temperament, reflecting side by side the concerns of family life (in the broadest meaning of the word) and social life and the need for a way of escape into dreams or meditation of a kind easy to imagine when visiting the Garden of Tranquil Longevity, a retreat for the aesthetic recreation of a monarch which Emperor Qianlong had laid out for him inside the Forbidden City.

The visitor today has only the brief moments of a scheduled tour in which to enjoy these gardens, effigies of the men of other times, sites the scholars brought into use and arranged for constant delight corresponding to their mood or social duties, year after year and following the cycle of the seasons. Gardens of a lifetime seen in a few hours.

It does not need much to retrieve some scraps of this old-fashioned atmosphere, between the community and the individual. It can sometimes be enough, for example, to stay for a while in a quiet hotel, like the one near Wuxi, not far from Suzhou, with a view over Lake Tai and a garden below the Western style hotel building. The layout of the garden, without any clear intention of reproducing famous gardens, recalls the private gardens of old. Listening from the summer house in the pond, in the warm spring twilight, to the loving converse of the frogs, or from another, hidden in a copse, to the morning song of the birds; glimpsing, as night falls, the black gleam of bamboo shoots stoutly pushing their way up through the soil, almost seeing their lightning growth; smelling, across the undulating slopes of hill and valley, the mingled scents of trees and shrubs in full flower, while stooping figures still sweep the leaves of the previous winter, heaping them up in large baskets like hoop nets; and somewhere, the cries of child-

ren playing ball. The hotel, big as a transatlantic liner, ceases to exist. A halt refreshing the mind before taking the road back to the scholars' gardens with the feeling of having shared some of their cherished delights.

Like their roofs jointed to withstand earthquake shocks, the Chinese residence is a combination of articulated blocks designed to fulfil different functions. The layout of the various buildings leaves space for the creation of little courtyards and intimate gardens. Like the residence, the garden does not seem to have been intended for an overall view but rather for a series of partial views. Some of the gardens seem at first sight to have been designed with an element of continuity patterned around an ornamental pool, but there is nothing "panoramic" about them; to photograph them with a wide-angle lens would be to misrepresent altogether their spatial projection. Their every feature is, on the contrary, so placed that at each move, compositions —or their details—hidden at first, come into view with an almost graphic play of contrasts and conflicting themes. The contrasts are, however, always subtle and the mild contradictions appear only at particular hours and seasons.

Peking, Beihai Park: Garden of the Retreat of the Painted Boat (Huafangzhai). Laid out in 1757, now being restored.

樹
繞
蒼
崖
溪

澗
凍
橋
閣
仙

居
家
上
層
不

橋
物
桃
間
點

絨
春
山
早
兄

氣
如
蒸
己
卯
春
月
渦
題

Silk scroll.

86

Peking, Forbidden City: Garden of the Palace of Tranquil
Longevity, from the Pavilion of Towering Beauty.

Yangzhou: Garden of the Shi Kefa Memorial Temple (Shigongci).

Yangzhou: Garden of the Small Winding Valley.

Movements and angles of vision

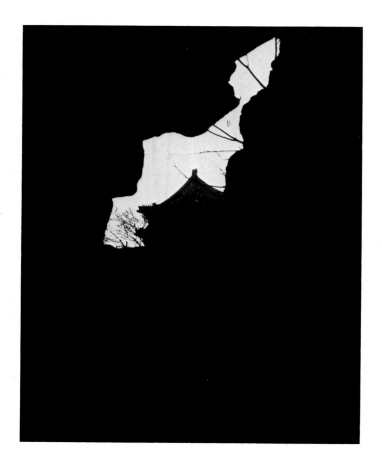

Distortion in time, distortion in space... Fifteen minutes' interval in a performance and a thousand years have passed; three strides to go from dawn to dusk. But the keen visitor, when the sun reaches the zenith, trains eye and lens on the whitewashed wall in order to fix the milky luminescence of the moon.

By their broken junctions the covered passages, before they lead to the main rooms, open up on their detours views of more intimate compositions. They form an indistinct frontier between the public and the private spheres, but the private sphere is still "domestic," belonging to the family, the clan. They are bounded on one side by a wall pierced with holes letting through the air, that is to say the Breath Force, and catch the eye with fleeting, centred and fragmented glimpses of the beyond, seen through successive geometrically shaped eyeholes revealing the feminine grace of a dancing stone, or soft or plant-like outlines framing rigidly vertical compositions.

Peking, Beihai Park:
Garden of the Serenity Study.

This sophistication of the angles of vision in Suzhou gardens was to influence the design of Chinese gardens throughout the Empire. Not without an element of scenic art, it also influenced some aspects of the theatre. Decor and transparency, making besides for excellent integration of the exterior (reconstructed nature) and the interior (the sheltered zone), also highlighted the difficulty of isolating the individual as he is understood in contemporary Western thought.

Leaving the covered passages and entering the stone universe of the garden, other openings are found and other angles of vision focussing on yet more distant views; for example, an empty space between two stones through which to glimpse the roofs of the Ten Buddhas Pagoda (p. 88).

Yangzhou: Garden of the Shi Kefa Memorial Temple.

Suzhou: Garden of the Green Wave Pavilion (Canglangting).

In his lectures Mr Chen Congzhou, professor of the history of architecture at the Tongji University in Shanghai, defines the two types of viewing that gardens call for: *in-position* (fixed point) and *in-motion* (which we have touched on in the previous pages). To explain the distinct nuances registered by the eye but not always analysed by the mind, although they underlie the rules of three-dimensional composition, he links up our way of observing a natural landscape and our way of looking at a painting: "Watching a distant mountain from a fixed point is like focussing one's eye on an album of paintings, while making a tour in a mountain is like unfolding a hand scroll before one's eyes. With one, the emphasis is on giving prominence to certain features of the scenery, with the other it is on the continuity and integration of scenery." So it is with the garden: it should be designed to favour now the one type of viewing, now the other type.

"In garden viewing, repose resides in motion and motion stems from repose. And from the interaction of the two an infinite variety of changing views come into being... To a person sitting in a pavilion, the racing clouds and flowing water, the flying birds and falling petals are all things in motion; whereas to a sailing boat or a strolling person, the hills, rocks, trees and woods are all things at a standstill... From the interaction of motion and repose, beauty naturally results... Hence we have the key to garden designing in the relationship between in-motion and in-position garden viewings." [9]

And, we may add, in the enclosed space of the garden will arise the possible choice of perceiving the movement of the Universe or evoking a journey.

Suzhou: Garden to Linger In (Liuyuan).

Suzhou: Lion Grove Garden.

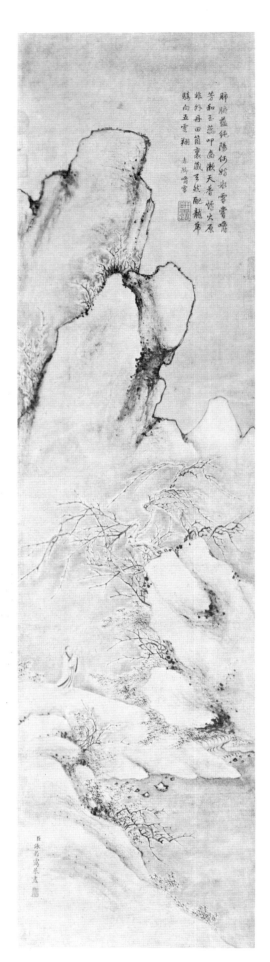

師順舊純陽仙始冰雪當噙
芳和玉蕊呷函漱天香嬈火原
非約丹田笛裏癀子欲配離爐
騎尚五雲翔
赤脚噴雪

Zhang Ruoai (1713-1746), Qing Dynasty:
Figure in the Snow.
Paper scroll.

This painting illustrates the theme of the iron-footed
Taoist, who is said to walk barefoot in the snow chewing
plum blossoms mixed with snow "in order to scent and
cool his entrails."

Paving of assembled waters

Girt with walls, the residence shut in on itself was a world to itself, a mass of passages, internal and domestic ways and secret gardens which the modern visitor seldom notices, or altogether misses if, as in the case of the Garden of the Master of the Fishing Nets, at Suzhou, the only access to the main garden is an almost completely hidden door to the north of the residence. That is how the visitor comes on this intimate corner with no room for a perspective view, in which the stone compositions have been designed to be seen from the living rooms, through the lattice-windows.

Some stones for an intimate garden, contemporary with this picture, illustrate the classical theme of the lone walker come from the mountain to replenish his spiritual resources from beneficent currents. Over the similarity in form of the mountain and this rock, raised stone and distant mountain, one can superimpose that of the theme of the spectator who has no doubt projected himself in thought, identified with the lone walker, at the foot of this rock where, between the two stones lying on the ground, the stream divides. The long bent grasses evoke the waterfall rich with the Breath Forces, here the paving of assembled waters.

Made of small round pebbles from the river, the paving is thus a stretch of water, its movement represented by geometric or floral patterns, or images of real or mythical animals (dragon or phoenix), or any other figure suggesting mobility. Contemporary gardeners working in mosaic feel the same need, even if they no longer understand why, when they insert figures of bicycles or cars in their designs, because water without movement, even represented by stones, bears with it the putrefaction of sickness and death.

Whatever the size of the garden or its stone compositions, the same ideas recur with the passage of time. If we stayed longer than other visitors looking at these simple stones, it was because we found ourselves suddenly looking at an almost familiar landscape, that of *kare san sui*, the "dry" gardens of the Kyōto monasteries.

Suzhou: Garden of the Master of the Fishing Nets.
North-east courtyard, cobble stones, plum blossom design.

The fired clay becomes brick,
the charred wood becomes charcoal,
the bees' nest becomes honey,
the froth of liquids becomes stone.
The whole results from the transformation
of the soft and shifting
into the hard and solid.

Ge Gong, an alchemist of the fourth century.

Yangzhou: Garden of the Resounding Roars Mountain Villa
(Jixiao Shanzhuang). Flagging.

THE GREAT RULE
OF THE METAMORPHOSIS
OF THE WORLD

Jin Tingbiao, Qing Dynasty: Playing the Flute at the
Enchanted Grotto. Paper scroll.

Fleeting spring

Peking, Forbidden City: Garden of the Palace of Tranquil Longevity. The "cup-floating stream" on the floor of the porch in the Pavilion of the Ceremony of Purification.

The influence of Taoism and Buddhism very early favoured the development of poetry reflecting in personal strain the attitude of man towards life and Nature expressed in sensitive comment on the weather according to the rhythm of the seasons. This poetry was to give rise to landscape painting.

"In the painting of scenes depicting the four seasons, the atmosphere varies, each having its own climate; it therefore becomes a matter of observing and analysing the weather and the seasons... [however] the variety of atmospheres cannot be limited to the simple scheme of the four seasons" (Shitao, Ch. XIV).

The scholars, familiarized by their duties with the Chinese countryside and steeped in ancient culture, in the course of their travels across a country as big as a continent gleaned many poetic emotions and, as soon as they settled anywhere, took pleasure in recreating, as far as their means allowed—using stone compositions or a few pebbles—the essence of the landscape scenes they had visited.

A traditional custom, observed even today, is that of visiting famous sites at particular times of the year, at the moment when vegetation and light set off their natural beauty to best advantage, or if they had been the scene of some historic or legendary event, at the time of its commemoration.

In his Garden of Tranquil Longevity in the Forbidden City, the Emperor Qianlong had carved out for him, in a stone slab sheltered by an open pavilion, the meanderings of the famous stream on whose banks the calligrapher poet Wang Xizhi (307-365?) once invited forty scholar friends for a drinking party ending with a competition in which they improvised poems to celebrate the spring.

In any garden, the role of vegetation is to evoke the annual round of the seasons, but in that of the scholar the play of stones, at one and the same time landscape and seasons, also expresses "the great rule of the metamorphosis of the world."

In the systems establishing the correspondence between the Elements, each season has its orientation, its element, its colour, and is symbolized in poetry by a flower:

Suzhou: Garden of the Master of the Fishing Nets.

WINTER / NORTH / WATER /
Black (of a sunless place) /
PLUM BLOSSOM

AUTUMN / WEST / METAL /   N   SPRING / EAST / WOOD /
White (after sunset void) / W—E Blue-green /
CHRYSANTHEMUM   S   PEACH BLOSSOM

SUMMER / SOUTH / FIRE /
Sun-flame red /
WHITE LOTUS

Spring, fleeting and violent, flamboyant outcome of long gestation, leaves behind it the desire to preserve its brief proliferation and the bright vision of it when the season has fled, the flowers have faded. The stones of spring therefore tend to be clear and slight to the verge of fragility. They are placed in such a way as to be lit by the rising sun with, as well as flowers and shrubs, a clump of bamboos to complete the setting, bamboos with rustling leaves whose colour, between blue and green, is the colour of spring. But some tapered greenish-grey stones are also bamboos and, grouped in the middle of a copse of real bamboos, seem likewise as unexpected and disproportionate as the young sprouts piercing the soil. The same stones will be found further on evoking again the "distant mountain" on the west side of the Garden of Serenity Study (Jingxinzhai) where, like all stones related to spring, they are sited so as to catch the first rays of the sun.

Some compositions bring spring and winter together using stones of different aspect (p. 15) in a play of contrasts; the real opposition is, however, not so much between winter (Yin) and summer (Yang) as between winter, marking the end of the downward cycle of the dragon, and spring, the beginning of his ascendant cycle with the progressive growth of the Yang element on the way to its full blossoming in summer.

◁ Peking, Forbidden City: Imperial Garden.

▷ Suzhou: Garden to Linger In.

▽ Suzhou: Garden of Harmony (Yiyuan).

Summer mountains

The summer composition is one of the most important as much for its grandiose development as for the symbols embodied in both its static prospect and movement, in distant as in nearer perspective, since this composition is also designed (the only one of its kind) to be entered.

In rural China summer is a time of intense activity. For the scholar, whether the climate is continental or tropical, it is a trying season. The least gesture is exhausting, the town is dank; if the scholar cannot get away, he devotes himself to dreaming of cool, breezy places and the freshness of the mountains. Only the favoured few can afford to represent this season in their garden; it needs ample space and a minimum of indispensable scenery, not the least item being the ornamental water.

The summer composition is not so much a representation of the mountain as a monumental rockery, a rock wall made of grouped stones in very marked relief. Whether the stones are, as at Suzhou and in some imperial gardens, brought from Lake Tai, or as at Yangzhou, for example, less baroque mountain stones, they all bear marks of erosion. In the way they are placed in the garden, this composition is sometimes confused with the protective barrier against the noxious currents from the north from which, according to the Fengshui rules, every home should be preserved.

The predominant vertical lines of the more or less projecting elements, limpid and almost white in colour, recall that summer corresponds to the south, full south, when the sun darts its rays down

Suzhou: Lion Grove Garden.

Yangzhou: Garden of the Small Winding Valley.

from the zenith and to the element of fire; and that the white lotus, the flower of summer, floats on the pool in which the wall is mirrored. The cinnabar red of the Taoist magicians is the colour of summer, but metal heated to incandescence is also said to be white hot.

The setting of the garden offers the spectator first of all the distant prospect since, for the purposes of orientation, he has to be separated from the composition by the water. This distant prospect makes movement hardly worthwhile; it is based on a fixed point, pavilion or residence, and it becomes the "image" of remote summer, chiefly in winter when the penetrating cold, whether dry or humid, makes one shiver. Then the prospect somehow warms the mind, if not the body. This distant contemplative prospect with the contrasts of light and shade and the trembling reflection in the water which doubles its height, brings the composition close to a landscape painting. And the same as the landscape painting it authorizes the mental journey into the interior of the mountain.

Yangzhou: Isolated Garden (Geyuan). Stone compositions on the north side of the pond.

Peking, Beihai Park: Garden of the Serenity Study. Stone compositions on the north side of the ornamental lake.

Yangzhou: Isolated Garden. Stone compositions on the north side of the pond.

Yangzhou: Isolated Garden.

The mountain scene painted by Wang Yun follows the classical division of vertical paintings in three registers. We liken it to the summer composition not because it really suggests this season, but because the theme of the persons situated at the mouth of the caves or on the point of going to them recalls that summer is the most favourable season for excursions to mountain cavities. Some of these caves and grottoes were the refuge of mythical beings or historical persons noted for their marginal existence, their desire to break with their time in order to attain wisdom and immortality or, more down to earth, to flee oppression and plot revolt.

Talking about Truth in a Jade Grotto. Woodcut after a painting by Wang Qiaoyun, from the *Yuchuyi*, a book of extraordinary stories, Ming Dynasty, 1606.

Just as it is difficult in this painting to follow the path that leads to the grotto in the upper register, the place where a saintly man is offering devotions to the Buddha, so no road appears at first sight to lead to the summer composition. To get there, it is necessary to go round a great part of the edge of the pool. Between two folds of the rock wall, in a part of it yet to be discovered, a gaping hole in the rock gives access to the interior of the mountain. On reaching this point, the spectator finds that he is really at the junction of two territories, on the borders of the solar and the subterranean forces. He touches this dragon's skin, these external veins of the earth, still half blinded by the reverberation. He begins to feel the cool air of the shadows. As his eyes grow accustomed to the darkness, he discerns in the play of internal reliefs, disturbing or soothing forms of sages, immortals, or demons that might emerge from them.

Wang Yun (1652-1735),
Qing Dynasty: Landscape.
Silk scroll.

106   Yangzhou: Western Garden (Xiyuan) of the Great Bright Temple (Daming si). Cliff by the pond.

Suzhou: Western Garden. Buddhist triad in the prayer room of the Jiedonglu Buddhist monastery. Gilt wood.

Peking, Forbidden City: Imperial Garden. Evocation of caverns.

Buddhism first penetrated into China by way of the caravans through the Central Asian oases, from the Indus Valley. The doctrine thus propagated was no longer that of early Buddhism, and the art it sponsored had already undergone both Iranian and Hellenistic influences. Together with the statuary, the building technique of the rock temples (i.e. the famous Bamyan caves north-east of Kabul) reached northern China between the 5th and 8th centuries. Work on the first cave temples of the Thousand Buddhas at Dunhuang is thought to have begun in A.D. 366. The great sites of Longmen, Maijishan, Binglingsi, Yungang and Dunhuang influenced all temple statuary: the Buddhas, the Bodhisattvas and all the figures of the Buddhist pantheon are in China usually represented in a sculptural setting (whether of stone, bronze or wood) which is reminiscent of the rock temples. In the Western Garden of the Great Bright Temple (Daming si) at Yangzhou, the high artificial cliff creates vast shadowy areas at its base, suggesting both the depth of the mountain and the ornamental niches housing the Buddhas; some stone compositions in the Imperial Garden also suggest them. These contrasts of light and shadow, peopled by the imagination with saints and sages, remind us that in early Buddhism it was the rule to represent only the surroundings or attributes of the Master. In early bas-reliefs the invisible Presence was signified by a harnessed but riderless horse, accompanied by a servant with a sunshade.

107

Autumn walks

"When hoar frost begins to whiten the fields [in the ninth lunar month] agricultural work comes to an end." [10]

The fierce heat has abated. The Yang accumulation gives birth to the Yin. The season for seeking shaded retreats is over. Now, on the contrary, the time begins for the last walks in the mountains, marked by a kind of feverish desire that this, too brief, fine season should not end. In ancient China autumn, together with spring, was the time for the conclusion of betrothals, the consummation of spring trysts. There was a suggestion of frenzy in the air. The last moments of the fine season had to be savoured to the full. "The Feast of the Double Nine, as its name indicates, fell on the ninth day of the ninth month. It was one of the oldest traditional festivals. Its significance and origins are uncertain; it seems to have commemorated the way an ancient people escaped from a natural catastrophe by taking refuge at the top of a mountain. Whatever its original meaning, it is still the custom on the Day of the Double Nine to climb a mountain, a hill, or any nearby height. The festival has become as well a pretext for an enjoyable excursion and picnic." [11]

In gardens, autumn stones are raised to evoke the season of walks on the heights when the desire for shaded retreats is already a thing of the past, replaced by the wish to enjoy the last warmth of the sun before winter comes. Whatever their size (at Geyuan, they form a massive block; at Shigongci they are more modest), the autumn compositions suggest climbing; the steep, rocky slopes with sharp ridges conceal in their folds stone steps giving access to the flattened summit. They appear at their best in the late afternoon, when the sun reddens the sky and the long shadows underscore the angular forms and open up deep gorges and bottomless ravines. In the distant prospect, the

◁△ Yangzhou: Isolated Garden. The autumn mountains east of the garden.

composition as a whole revives memories of marvellous autumn excursions.

There is no danger of being mistaken in attributing to autumn all compositions in which the summits to be reached are levelled; it will also be noted that they are so oriented as to receive the sun's rays from the west.

In the decoration of interior courtyards, the stone evoking autumn is recognized by its angular form and almost horizontal upper part.

乙酉九章夏六月獻生鴻泰溪馮觀文群為竹石鞠君茂平不礙雲山樓

◁ Attributed to Ma Wan (fl. 1342-1366),
Yuan Dynasty:
Secluded Dwelling amid Lofty Peaks,
1349. Silk scroll.

▷ Yangzhou: Isolated Garden.
The autumn mountains east
of the garden.

112   Yangzhou: Isolated Garden. The winter mountain south of the garden.

Winter visions

The stones of spring are boisterous, those of summer are incandescent and those of autumn, proud and nostalgic. The cycle of the seasons is completed by recollection and gestation; nature lapses into lethargy, man huddles himself up in his quilted robes. Still very strong in the autumn stones, the Yang forces fade, leaving room for the soft and languishing Yin forces in the winter stones.

Facing the north aspect of the mountain, whose slopes are never in the sun, the winter compositions are modest compared with the magnificence of those of summer or autumn; they can be raised in the corner of a patio, to be seen from the residence. Sometimes bamboo-shoot stones, a note of hope for milder days, are placed in the foreground.

In their winter compositions, representing the season when all plant, animal and human life suddenly disappears from the fields, the stone raisers have also expressed the two key concepts of Chinese philosophy and cosmology: Plenitude and Void. "Far from being mutually exclusive, their close marriage forms the warp and woof of the world; thus, the void is a negative notion, synonymous with absence, but it also reveals the essence of things (in the examples given by Laozi, the void is the hub that lets the wheel turn, the emptiness of the pitcher that makes it useful and the open spaces of the door and windows that make a room serviceable).

"As these two concepts play such an important role in the philosophical description of the world, it is not surprising that they should be found in the forefront, on the one hand, of theories of painting, and on the other hand, of theories of the garden, since the two disciplines are precisely, at microcosmic level, a replica of the creative act that gave birth to the Universe. In painting, fullness and emptiness form the very substance of plastic space; the white blanks on the paper are more important than the painted parts, but they only take their value and their positive meaning from the existence of the latter; the essential is implied but it only exists by virtue of what is expressed. The two terms (the unexpressed and the expressed, blank and painted parts, empty and full) have therefore identical substance and cannot be separated." [12]

This long quotation from Pierre Ryckmans' note in his translation of Shen Fu's *Six Stories as the Fickle Days Go By* is given here because these two concepts are very clearly expressed in many winter compositions. The rocks are systematically placed so as to stand out against the background of a white wall quite close behind them when they are not directly embedded in it; they seem to emerge from the very void and look like matter in momentary lethargy, whose energy flows might soon be ready to stir. The winter compositions, more than other monochrome compositions, come nearest to the scholars' paintings where all shades of meaning are expressed in ink of varying density spread on the white paper background.

Yangzhou: Garden of the Resounding Roars Mountain Villa. The uprush of spring against a winter background.

Yangzhou: Garden of the Resounding Roars Mountain Villa.   115

Attributed to Zhou Wenju, Southern Tang (Five Dynasties):
Watching the Ducks at the Water Pavilion, c. 970.
Fan, silk album leaf.

"A mountain is there for the climbing and it is good if the climber can take a short pause at intervals and look around. This is why in ancient times the general practice was to lay stone steps up a hill. This suited the physical build of the human body that is accustomed to an erect posture. Now stone steps have been replaced by sloping roads which in fact are not only less safe but may even kill the fun of climbing... Roads should be winding rather than straight. If it can be made that narrow paths and trails will predominate over main roads, then there will be numerous spots of seclusion and the tourists will be able to scatter all over the area. They will look for their own favourite retreats where they can linger around, listening to the tinkle of springs, taking short rests on rocks or lapsing into a contemplative mood and giving play to their poetic impulses."
Chen Congzhou, *On Chinese Gardens*, 1985.

NEAR STONES,
FAR MOUNTAINS

Hong Ren (1610-1663), Qing Dynasty: Dragon Pine on the Yellow Mountain.

Gu Kaizhi (346-407): The Nymph of the River Luo.
Copy of the 12th or 13th century. Section of the silk scroll.

The poet forsaken by the nymph

On a horizontal scroll, the painter Gu Kaizhi (346-407) illustrated the poem *The Nymph of the River Luo*. This twelfth century copy (it is not unique, there are at least two others, in the Peking and Shenyang museums) depicts the poet abandoned by the river deity, dreaming, disconsolate, beside the river. "The elements of the landscape —hills, rocks, trees—still preserve their character as images; conceived individually, they are juxtaposed as one would arrange ready-made stage props, without much concern for size relationships or placement in space... The figures are disproportionately large, perhaps because the story is still the prime consideration of the painter." [13]

In this same period, Zong Bing (375-443), a painter whose works have all been lost, wrote: "Given that the Kunlun Mountains are very big and the pupil of the eye is very small, if the mountain is brought within an inch of my eyes, I cannot see its shape; but if it is moved several miles away, it can be held in the pupil of my eyes. For the further away the object, the smaller it becomes. Now, when I spread the silk to reflect a distant landscape, the shape of the Kunlun and Lang Mountains can be contained in the space of a square inch." [14] In this way, he created another form of pictorial symbolism in which man no longer predominated by his size but filled a more realistic place at the heart of the surrounding nature, and this made it possible to give a clearer representation of the systems relating Heaven, Earth and men—systems already very old at that time—so that the Chinese landscape, more than reflecting a state of mind, became an expression in pictorial terms of a philosophical attitude.

Commenting on this picture of the poet abandoned by the nymph, James Cahill has written: "Neither the painter's technical means nor his power of visualization were adequate to suggest, at least to the modern viewer, the animistic world of Zong Bing's text, in which plants, streams and rocks are endowed with spiritual essences and captivate the soul of man. Still less could he call forth any sense of the grand and pervasive movement which unites the Taoist cosmos into a single organism." But, he adds, "the viewer of a painting responds to familiar conventions with a directness denied to those who find them strange; the mushroom-like trees and modest hillocks of this naïvely presented scene were no doubt metamorphosed, in the eyes of the early nature-lover, into dense forests and towering peaks." [15]

From the way this detail appears, it has to be asked whether it should be regarded as the representation of a landscape or of a landscape as it would be expressed in the space of a garden.

Comparing this scene with the model of the Tang garden (p.64), similar disproportions can be seen between the persons in the one and the birds perched on the "mountain" in the other. These observations suggest that it is not so much naïveté in expression as the desire to represent something else. The abandoned poet might well be imagined to be in a garden in which he would have recreated the surroundings of his melancholy adventure, in between a pool bordered by willows and a representation of the distant mountain, with in the foreground the flow of petrified water undulating like a dragon, the entire painting bathed in the symbolic colours of the Yin/Yang equilibrium.

Climbing the mountain

The lesson of the long road to travel in order to reach the heights, to attain purity and detachment from the things of the world, is represented in painting by this little person standing at the foot of the mountain, at the meeting of currents, in the place known as the Dragon's Lair. Transferred to the garden, this pictorial expression of an environment is recreated, regardless of the objective dimensions of the elements set in place for the purposes of a projection in this medium.

The waterside pavilion is the starting point of the mental ascent; the scholar loses himself in his dreams, his lute beside him, while raindrops beat down on the large banana leaves, providing inspiration for the accompaniment of a poem. Withdrawn from the world, motionless, in the limpid twilight he contemplates the changing scene. Whether his mountain is a luxuriant slope or a stone composition barely higher than himself, the feelings it is going to rouse will be the same evocation of man's destiny in the Universe, and reminiscences of joyous climbs during which, drinking tea or wine, life was lived in communion with nature.

I cannot see those who went before me.
I cannot see those who will come after me.
I dream of the infinity of the universe.
Alone and sad, I let my tears flow.

Wang Shen, Northern Song Dynasty: Misty Landscape of Tiered Mountains and Rivers. Silk scroll.

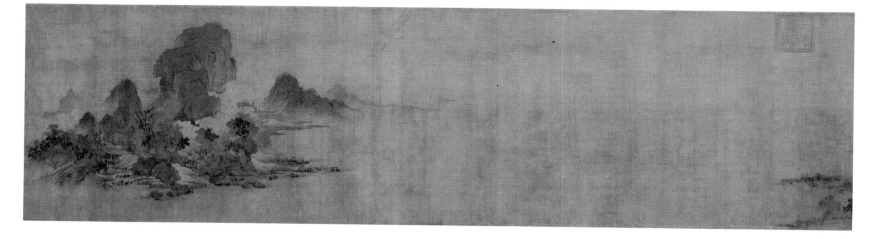

Peking, Beihai Park: Garden of Serenity Study. Upward way to the Zhenluan belvedere.

Peking, Beihai Park: One approach to the Garden of the Painted Boat Retreat.

Did the scholar in his garden recall these verses written by the poet Chen Ziang (661-702) after his climb to the Youzhou Belvedere?

Visitors to the scholars' gardens today (gardens remodelled in many cases by rich businessmen at the end of the eighteenth century, but for whom they would have been abandoned) see in them only the reflection of social success and accumulated treasures, forgetful of other gardens, such as the one constructed by the painter Shitao at Yangzhou, of which practically nothing remains.

In the mental ascent, motionless exercise at the lowest level of the composition in the painting as in the garden, the scholar is still the lay person who belongs to the century he contemplates. When, however, he wishes to identify himself with the personages who in the paintings climb the mountainside alone to reach isolated constructions resembling places of retreat, or Buddhist monasteries, he goes to his garden to carry out physically this wholly mental exercise.

The slope seen from the pavilion looks like an insurmountable barrier; it can however be skirted, revealing among a number of simulated obstacles, labyrinthine paths reducing the scale of both time and space.

Garden mountains, dream mountains, whose ascent can only be made alone between narrow rifts, which recall mountain paths.

This displacement, become for a brief moment physical, sets the entire landscape in a new frame. In one garden or another, steps to be climbed afford fleeting views at points provided for a halt to take breath, so that having reached a ledge, a terrace or a belvedere, inviting contemplation of a panoramic view, the gaze no longer turns towards the garden, the spaces just left behind, but towards other compositions, suddenly discovered or, if already visible from some other part of the garden, having acquired here another meaning.

▷ Yangzhou: Western Garden (Xiyuan) of the Great Bright Temple (Daming si).

王蒙瓣用古篆隸法雜入皴中。如金鑚鏤沙。石鶴嘗劃沙。雜師趙吳興實自出鑪冶。犬而不稗勁而不板圖而不成毛圍方而不露圭角。其英唐宋諸家無不一一逼肖元李推爲第一大凡學一人不可苑在一人園如叔明者其於諸家眞毫髮無遺憾矣。

Plate from Wang Gai's
Mustard Seed Garden Manual of Painting, 1679.

▷ Peking: Zhongshan Park (Sun Yat-sen Memorial).

Peking: Zhongshan Park (Sun Yat-sen Memorial).

Zhou Chen (1450-1535), Ming Dynasty: Leisurely
Watching Children Collect Willow Flowers.

*Illustrating the last line of a quatrain by the Southern
Song poet Yang Wanli (1124-1206), entitled "After the
Early Summer Nap":*

>*The plums have lost the sourness that made my teeth tingle.*
>*Outside my windows the banana trees show me their green leaves.*
>*A long day and I rise carefree from my nap*
>*And leisurely I watch children collecting willow flowers.*

Suzhou: Lion Grove Garden.

The mountain contemplated

The summer house or belvedere on the mountain has a very different function from that of the pavilion at the foot of it, although it can be similar in form. That is secondary. Just as in landscape paintings, the upper third always looks inaccessible to man, and any buildings portrayed are placed at the level of the second third, so the mountain summer house is never set on the summit of a stone composition but only on the semblance of a summit, in order to show that the space occupied by the mountain does not end there and another foreground is going to appear between man and outer space.

Facing the scholar seated in his belvedere, a summit emerges, a summit he will not climb. He fixes it with his human gaze; no road leads there and furthermore, beyond this first forbidden peak there appear, in a distance so far from objective that three arm's lengths could reach them, dizzy rocky heights, supremely remote peaks which, as for example at Jingxinzhai, surge upwards in the northwest corner, as though at the junction of winter and spring or situated on the borders of the inhabited lands of the Empire.

I built my house among men
but no sound of horse or carriage disturbs me.
How can that be?
In the remote heart, every place is a retreat. [16]

I lived for a long time in a cage.
Here I am at last given back to myself.
Poems of Tao Yuanming (365-427)

Whether he is alone, in nature, facing the mountain, or whether he retires, alone in his garden, before the rocks he has put up, he contemplates and interrupts time.

Attributed to Ren Renfa (1254-1327), Yuan Dynasty: A Lofty Scholar Playing the Lute. Silk scroll.

Yangzhou: Garden of the Small Winding Valley.

Peking, Forbidden City: Taihu stone on base in the courtyard
of the Palace of Inheriting Heaven.

Yangzhou: Isolated Garden.

Zhou Chen (1450-1535), Ming Dynasty:
Arrival of a Visitor at a Mountain Hermitage. Silk scroll.

"As soon as we stand still, we are elsewhere, dreaming in an unbounded world. Boundless is the movement of the still man. Boundlessness is one of the dynamic characteristics of quiet withdrawal...
"In such reveries as take hold of the meditating man, the details fade away, the picturesque loses colour, the hour sounds no more, and time stretches away limitlessly."

Gaston Bachelard, *L'Intuition de l'Instant*.

THE MOVEMENT OF STONES

Wuxi: Plum Garden (Meiyuan).

Faraway Thoughts While Leaning on the Balustrade. Woodcut after a painting by Wang Qiaoyun, from the *Yuchuyi*, a book of extraordinary stories, Ming Dynasty, 1606.

Clouds carve mountains

However imaginary it may be, the journey needs the support of material images representing instants in time and atmospheric changes. Whoever observes the course of clouds in the mountains, the wreaths of mist isolating the summits and filling the valleys, is familiar with the transformations undergone by mountains.

"Clouds, recapitulation of the landscape," writes Hubert Damisch, and goes on to quote Nicole Vandier-Nicolas: "For in their elusive void many mountain traits can be seen and many veiled modes of water; that is why people talk of mountains of clouds, oceans of clouds." In their treatises, the role painters gave to clouds was "that of an element, a principle which, according to whether it is assembled or dispersed, forms with its 'elusive void' the bond of the landscape, articulating and at the same time disguising the 'mountain traits' and 'modes of water'." [17]

Many scholar painters from the most ancient times were theorists of painting. [18] Discussing landscape, they discussed mountains; discussing mountains, they spoke of clouds; in their pictorial

works they covered sheet after sheet, their brushes more or less heavy with ink, or their fingers impregnated with special powders to be spread by their breath, expressing the infinite play of the two elements.

We have referred freely to Pierre Ryckmans' commentary on the *Remarks on Painting by the Monk Bitter Pumpkin*, for this reason: since the Zen gardens in Japan are known to have been created by monks who were great calligraphers and painters, we have assumed that the scholar's garden was from the first made by scholars, as these are defined and met with again as authors of treatises on painting. We know that Shitao, painter and theorist, built gardens, and we are entitled to think he was not the only one or the first to do so. Starting from there, we can therefore take it that the creators who knew how to theorize about clouds also knew how to find for their gardens—recreating imaginary nature—stones, all cavities and hollows, that were the most apt to express this relation of water (in all its forms) to the mountain (that is to say, eroded stones taken from Lake Tại) and represent the infinity of changes undergone by the mountain. In this way they could use matter to reproduce the vaporous ascending dragons, the sheets of void they had captured in their paintings.

In Chinese characters, it should be remembered, landscape paintings are named "Mountain and Water."

Peking, Summer Palace (Yiheyuan): Detail of a monolith standing in the courtyard of the eastern entrance.

Peking, Forbidden City: Garden of the Palace of Tranquil Longevity.
"Cloud-catching" rock at the entrance of the Pavilion
of Expected Luck.

Suzhou: Garden to Linger In.

▷ Li Tang (1050-1130), Song Dynasty: Whispering Pines in the
Mountains, 1124. Silk scroll.

134   Suzhou: Lion Grove Garden. Stones from Lake Tai before the Cloud-Dwelling Pavilion (Woyunting).

Peking, Forbidden City: Imperial Garden.

Suzhou: Lion Grove Garden.

Alarm in the Monastery.
Plate from the *Xixiangji* published during
the Chongzhen period, Ming Dynasty,
between 1628 and 1643.

"Looking at the wreaths of fog, do the stones
fade away; and does the Void more than the Fullness take shape?

"Tell me, do you read there only the course of
the clouds?"

Facing the Chinese mountains, Victor Segalen,
a sea-loving Breton, cried out:

"Encircle me with your static swell, oh fixed sea!
oh tide without ebb! Sterile waves whose summits
join the dome of the skies embracing the whole of
my gaze."

And Shitao wrote:

"But he who only perceives the Sea to the prejudice of the Mountain, or the Mountain to the
prejudice of the Sea, in truth has only a blunted
perception."

Wang Meng (1309-1385): Forest Dwellings at Zhu Chu
(another name for Lake Tai). Paper scroll.

To seek to capture the meaning of stones is therefore a vast undertaking. It might be better to grasp the moment, and recreate the image of that moment in contemplating them.

Wreaths of mist can likewise change their form and stir other memories. There is no recipe, no definition of each stone; there are only moments they are brought to suggest. The moments they can evoke are not, however, really suggested by them but by the person who looks at them and discerns the significance of their movements, the movement for which they were chosen by the one who arranged them. His choice was never made with only one point of view in mind, but rather to propose a gamut of suggestions drawing on different stone materials, each more apt than the others to express the imaginary infinite.

One of Wang Meng's last works, dedicated to his friend Ri Zhang, portrayed in retirement with his wife and servants in pavilions lying near the caves at the foot of the Western Mountain, one of the islands in Lake Tai.

Suzhou: Lion Grove Garden.

Suzhou: Garden of Harmony (Yiyuan).

The Isles of the Immortals

Suzhou: Garden of the Green Wave Pavilion.

Peking, Forbidden City: Courtyard of the Palace of Inheriting Heaven.

Unlike the Japanese masters who kept to the principle of firm anchorage in earth and tended to give visual expression to the upward thrust of land from the abysmal depths of the ocean, the Chinese masters of the Gardens of Longevity seemed to reject any laws assuring stability and do their utmost to eliminate the weight of matter.

In the dawn of prehistory, mountains were thought to have broken loose and fallen from the dome of heaven to lie on the earth in chains of scree, as they are often depicted in stone raisers' compositions and landscape paintings. The Chinese, a people of farmers, were profoundly attached to the land, for them the sea was a far-off unsure expanse, a landless horizon which some bold spirits had discovered, but which had never seemed an indispensable element of Chinese life. Water was more often portrayed in rivers than in the sea. Excess was characteristic of Chinese rivers and their immoderate action had a large place in legend as well as history. Stories about the sea were rare; an outlet for continental waters, it appeared as the remote phase in the re-creation of the water-evaporation cycle.

"On the ocean horizon, the breath of sea monsters seems to erect towers [of foam]" (Sima Qian, *Historical Memoirs*). [19]

The distant sea became a mythical zone possibly concealing fabulous islands, the refuge of flying demons said to be able to distil the elixir of immortality, islands that might also, perhaps, have fallen from the dome of heaven, but on water instead of land. They were indeed said to be floating and, unstable owing to their giddy height, in constant danger of sinking into the ocean depths. That was why the Lord of Heaven, in the early days of Creation, had asked the giant turtles to take them on their back. These fabulous islands, five in all, were thus borne up by fifteen turtles on the waters of Bohai Gulf, between China and Korea. A passing giant had devoured six of the turtles and two of the islands sank for good. The three others, Penglai, Yingzhou and Fanghu, were still the home of the legendary distillers whom men, particularly the Emperors, were anxious to meet. In the third century B.C., the founder of the Qin dynasty sent

Yangzhou: Isolated Garden. In the foreground, the Isle of the Immortals.

thousands of young people with a team of Feng-shui masters to look for them, but they could not find them. The chronicles relate that Emperor Wu of the Han dynasty made two more unsuccessful attempts, in 133 and 109 B.C. These failures led him to try another approach. He had two lakes dug in the garden of his palace and built three islands in them, modelled on legendary descriptions and sail-ors' stories, in the hope that the spiritual beings would be willing to settle there. Later, some sailors discovered an archipelago of myriads of islands in the fog-bound eastern seas. They thought they had at last discovered the marvellous islands, but they only found there a "people of bare-footed dwarfs," the Japanese.

Emperor Wu had set the example. After him the Chinese continued to make images of these inac-cessible floating islands, places of refuge for Im-mortals and spirits who, by distilling the herbs of immortality, knew how to brew the mythical elixir, and raised narrow-based stones to recreate an im-pression of giddy height and instability. These re-presentations of islands had so little to do with the sea that, in course of time, the stone raisers simply replaced the liquid element by stone-bases with stereotyped designs symbolizing water or else set up the stones on low rocks suggesting giant turtle-backs.

While in Japan the evocation of the sea forms part of the garden, in China it is scarcely ever to be found. For the Chinese scholar, frequently on the move, over a country of vast extent, the sea was simply an outer boundary. "A pagoda stands by the waterside. There I went one evening with my fath-er—it was the mid-autumn festival—to watch the rising tide."[20] When the author, Shen Fu, tells of going to the mouth of the river Qiantang, in Hang-zhou bay, it was not particularly for a glimpse of the sea, but to witness the tidal bore which, at the autumn equinox, sets the waves surging and may sweep them up to a height of thirty feet. This nat-ural phenomenon had attracted Chinese tourists since remote times, and two emperors had made the journey in order to admire the sight.

Peking, Zhongshan Park (Sun Yat-sen Memorial).

Peking, Forbidden City: Courtyard of the Palace of Inheriting Heaven.

Peking, Summer Palace: Courtyard of the east entrance.

Suzhou: Garden of the Master of the Fishing Nets (left).
Western Garden of the Hanshan Temple (right).

Yun Ying Appearing in a Dream.
Woodcut after a painting by Wang Qiaoyun, from the
Yuchuji, a book of extraordinary stories, Ming Dynasty, 1606.

Suzhou: Garden of the Master of the Fishing Nets.

In immediate proximity to garden pavilions or within the small courtyards of residences, it was customary to raise stones evoking the stereotyped image of mythical islands. The reason lies in the belief that such stones could encourage the descent of Immortals to earth. Among the objects in the room, all of them symbolic in various ways, one notes the small vase on the right side of the print. Its broken line pattern may be compared with that of the opening made in a wall of the Lion Grove Garden (p. 138). This motif is a classical representation of the moment when water freezes into ice—the image of an ever changing world.

145

The cosmic dance

The moment in the life of the sea represented by a wave was captured by the masters of gardens and embodied by them in selected stones expressing the powerful upward thrust of the liquid mass. Like a photographer working to the thousandth of a second, they caught without congealing it, the movement of the crest on the point of falling back again.

Just as the whole idea of the sea is contained in this wave, so other stones can portray whirlpools in rivers, showers of spray and drops falling from them.

Water, air and vapour: in other compositions, from a mountainside sketched in by a few flat rocks, unfolding scrolls release the dragon of this water evoked by long grasses lying on the ground. That is when the stone becomes spiritualized in an image of vapours rising, then swelling and spreading through space before they mingle with the ether. This mushroom-shaped stone (p.148) might equally well call to mind one of the magic mushrooms able, according to the ancient Taoists, to give anyone eating it five hundred years of life. (See the model of the Tang garden, p.64.)

Peking, Summer Palace: Courtyard of the east entrance before the Pavilion of Benevolence and Longevity.

Peking, Forbidden City: Imperial Garden.

▷ Suzhou: Garden of the Master of the Fishing Nets.

Suzhou: Garden of the Master of the Fishing Nets.

Peking, Summer Palace: Courtyard of the east entrance before the Pavilion of Benevolence and Longevity. Top of a stone.

According to Joseph Needham, Confucianism, expressing a certain rational order and morality in a feudal state of society, is profoundly masculine; the "axis of the world" stones (p.37) collected by the emperors are masculine stones. In their search for intuitive wisdom, the Taoist philosophers rejected all preconceived ideas of a social order and "emphasized the feminine as the symbol of a receptive, specifically Taoist approach to nature." [21]

In contrast to the "axis of the world" stones collected by the Emperors, "masculine" stones, dark rocks with sharp angles, craggy and rough-hewn like a rugged face, the stones taken from Lake Tai were eroded by water, with often a very narrow base, so that they seemed barely to touch the ground and had the air of a ballet dancer.

The stones from Lake Tai are dancing and effeminate, those from the north all angles and shadows; some from mountain screes show the earth's geological strata in their veins, traces of the telluric folds of Creation, others evidence fusions and transformations; others again are strange

148

Gazing at the Moon on a Fine Evening.
Plate from the *Hongfuji*, a book of extraordinary tales,
2 volumes, Ming Dynasty, 1601.

Suzhou: Garden to Linger In.
Rock known as the Cloud-Capped Peak.

This monolith, sixteen and a half feet high, and the one known as the Cloud-Nestling Peak (see p. 23) both came from Lake Tai. Tradition has it that, while they were being shipped to the Song capital to be offered to an emperor, the boat sank in the lake. It was only several centuries later that they were set up in this garden.

149

minerals, fossilized wood, limestone nodules, meteorites from across space. In the garden, however, all of them, juxtaposed or brought together by the artist, take part in the dance of Creation.

Bhubaneswar (Orissa province, India): Temple of Mukteswar. Shiva dancing, 10th century.

Rhythm and movement, long deemed in the West to be qualities proper to the cycle of the seasons and of the birth and death of all living creatures, are likewise the very essence of inorganic matter, and from this fact "all matter here on earth or in space takes part in a continual cosmic dance." [22] In Hinduism the metaphor of the cosmic dance had been expressed in the dance of Shiva, god of Creation and Destruction, in this twofold simultaneous action.

In his dance, the conqueror of the three citadels
places his powerful foot on the earth gently
lest the earth be shattered by the shock;
he raises his arms and keeps them folded on his breast,
arms into which all the worlds could sink;
he turns away from visible objects, fearful of consuming them,
his gaze emitting terrible sparks.
May it protect you,
this divine dance,
made terrible by the mercy
the King of the world shows to all his Empire.

Viçakhadatta, sixth century

Ancient Chinese thought also had this intuition, confirmed by modern physicists, that change and transformation, that is to say rhythm and movement, are the basic substance of nature. That the distinction between solid, liquid and gaseous states is only the reflection of a difference in the speed of electrons, was something the artist stone raisers were aware of without being able to formulate it when with the aid of mineral matter they expressed these states and allowed the garden as a whole to express the concept of nature so that they could steep themselves in it and recover what the Taoist masters regarded as primeval spontaneity.

The garden stones evoked grandiose landscapes of the land of China in which the first masters of the Winds and Waters (Fengshui) had girded the pulsations of the Earth, the veins of the dragon, the currents of energy, in the undifferentiated folds of the rocks, the trajectory of the waters or the knots of trees.

These stones of cosmic movement, stones of waves and vapours, no longer the painted re-creation of landscapes, but a condensation of reality; these long sought stones, chosen and arranged in accordance with criteria which we must assume to have included some form of magic, were made by the scholar for himself, his close companions and perhaps for the visitors who contemplate his creations today, to the end that they might become fantastic elements capturing and giving forth real energy, emanations of the Breath Forces, and in this way make the space containing them the Garden of Longevity.

Peking, Zhongshan Park (Sun Yat-sen Memorial).

Suzhou: Great Pagoda of the Temple of Gratitude
(Baoen si), rebuilt in 1162.

From what forsaken garden came this stone now set at the foot of the
pagoda? No one could tell us, but just as it was found it was set
up here like a tower of foam and reiterates the dizzy ascent of the
building's nine levels. A contemplation stone for purposes of mental
ascent, for steeping oneself in the movement of the stones of China
before fathoming the movement of the stones of an archipelago whose
famous sites owe much to the sea.

THE OMNIPRESENT SEA

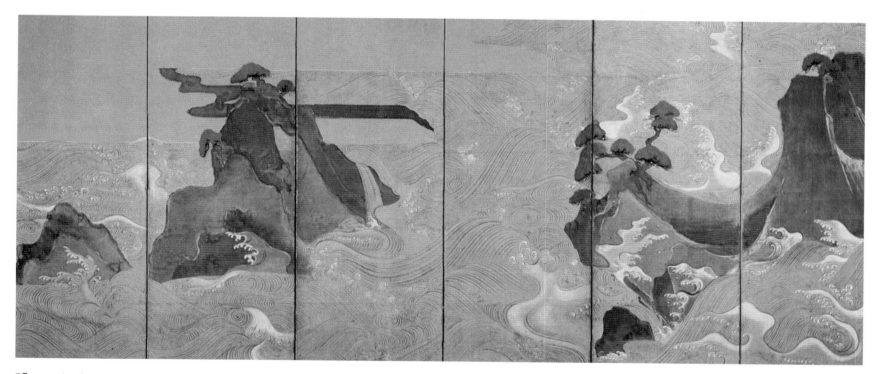

Sōtatsu (active c. 1630): Pine Islands (Matsushima).
Right side of a screen painting.

Kyōto: Shimogamo Shrine.

On certain feast days the Shinto priests set up models of these primordial mountains: bright white pointed cones standing in an area of white gravel—a conventional representation of the sea.

Crystallization

"Then the god Izanagi and the goddess Izanami stood on the Floating Bridge of Heaven; they plunged the divine halberd into the sea, stirred it round in the marine salt and pulled it out making the water plash. At that very moment, the salt drops that fell from the halberd, superposed on the surface, became islands" (*Kojiki*).

The Chinese mountains emerged from the Cosmic Ocean; those of Japan were only the crystallization of a very real sea. In both countries the Vital Flow descended from Heaven to the Earth passing by the tops of the mountains, but the currents of energy did not follow the same course. In China, the Flow came from the remote mountains in the West; in Japan, they came direct, vertically down.

In each village, a Shinto temple situated on a height is the site of the descent of the tutelary *Kami*, the divine spirit. The ritual consists in bidding, praying the spirit to come so that men can be regenerated in contact with its energy; then in accompanying it back to the holy site whence it takes flight back to the celestial spheres.

"According to the cosmology of the ancient Japanese, the universe is full of spiritual substances which, despite their immaterial and invisible

154

existence, have their own unity, their supernatural strength, their own feelings, and are able to fly through the air and take on any form they choose.

"All spiritual substances are classified in two categories, good and bad spirits, or purity and impurity. All material existences are likewise grouped in one or the other category, things containing felicitous elements and others possessed of evil spirits, or rather the pure and the impure.

"Furthermore, it seems to me that there are spiritual substances that are essentially good or bad. The most outstanding example of a consistently good spiritual substance is the ancestral spirit venerated as the founder-god of a group. His only concern is to give the greatest possible happiness to the group made up of his descendants. On the other hand, spirits of men or animals who died in strife, in an accident, in great anger or great sorrow, seek only to harm everyone they meet. Many spirits, however, are neither essentially good nor essentially bad, they are good when they are happy, bad when they are angry.

"Every community has a kind of eternal fund of good spirits. This is chiefly the symbol of the founder-god of the community, carefully housed in a temple; sometimes a particular water, stone or tree is a supplementary source. The spirits given off by these sources spread through the environs. They are also able to possess and dwell in bodies they meet. If a body invested with a good spirit comes into contact with another body, the spirit passes into the second body, in the same way as the current from an electrified body passes through a conducting body coming into contact with it.

"The same phenomenon takes place with evil spirits. This shows that gods and demons are made of the same substance. The two categories of spirits are, however, incompatible; the one chases the other away as an army repels the enemy. The territory occupied by a group of men always contains both elements; if the good element is stronger than the evil one, the prosperity of the group will be assured, but if the evil element predominates, the outlook for the group will be sombre...

"For the ancient Japanese, the universe was made of two elements, a spiritual and a material element. The two collide, mingle, neutralize or strengthen each other according to their mutual relations. It is in any case impossible for a man to live quite alone without any form of divine protection against the attacks of the evil spirits. But despite the dangers surrounding us, there is no reason to be alarmed because the dangerous influence of the evil spirits can be repulsed by the equally powerful forces at our disposal in the form of fetishes, divine objects, holy persons (priests, men belonging to traditionally venerable families), saints, etc."
(Narimitsu Matsudaira). [23]

Kyōto, Katsura Detached Palace Garden: Stone composition evoking the maritime site of Ama-no-hashidate.

Burial mound of the Emperor Sujin (5th century), Nara prefecture, photographed from the air.

Imported dragons

The tombs of the first Japanese Emperors, from the fourth to the seventh century, in the Yamato region, reflect the islanders' knowledge of telluric geomancy. The tomb of Sujin, mentioned in the chronicles as the tenth Emperor but identified now as the real founder of the centralized government, stands on an isolated eminence, remodelled by man, the last foothill of a chain of mountains. Surrounded by a moat, this tomb, a hemispheric island, has in front of it a trapezoidal area where the ritual ceremonies for the reception of the Spirit took place. The spirit of the dead, in this case the Emperor, could get to heaven by climbing the mountain chain and come down again vertically to the top of the eminence. Incidentally, the site for the reception of divine spirits is called a *niwa*, a term also used today for a garden.

From time immemorial, the Japanese have placed stones in the vicinity of Shinto shrines, round white pebbles surrounding the altars, or piles of rocks at the foot of holy trees. These compositions were held to favour the descent of the spirits of ancestors, clan chieftains or tutelary divinities. The country as a whole was, and is still, placed under the protection of *kamis*, who in order to visit their domain are liable to set foot on the top of any mountain, hill or mound suitably arranged by men, or any stones raised in conformity with ritual prescriptions.

The dragons of the Middle Empire, whose comings and goings so clearly reflected conditions in China, were going, as can be imagined, to have some difficulty in establishing themselves in the Archipelago. For the Japanese, surrounded on all sides by the sea and living at the foot of their mountains, the White Tiger of the Himalayan massifs in the West was as devoid of meaning as the Green Dragon of the Eastern Seas. In writing the *Sakutei-ki*, the Book of Secrets for the Use of Stone Raisers, the author, faced with the invasion of Chinese ideas, tried to sort out those that could be adopted without any danger, those it would be better to reject, and finally those that would have to be adapted to Japanese conditions. The last included the orientation rules governing the movement of the Water Dragon. In China, all the rivers come down from the snow-covered mountains in the West, the White Tiger, and flow into the Eastern Sea, symbolized by the Green Dragon, but that is no reason to run counter to the laws that govern the movement of the vital forces in Japan.

"At Tenno-ji, the water comes from the West and flows towards the East; at Kōyasan, the water also comes from the West. This is a special case, because it concerns temples; indeed, it [the water] symbolizes the introduction of Buddhism coming from India, thus from the West... Water can therefore come from the West, but only in temples, not for residences." Several times the author of *Sakutei-ki* repeats that in the case of residences "water comes from the *dragon* and must flow towards the *tiger*," and he specifies further as a "General Rule" that "from East to West... the best orientation is from the *dragon* to the *tiger*, then the master of the house will enjoy good health and long life." There is no doubt that here he is recalling a native tradition, dating from before the arrival of Buddhism.

▷ Suzhou: Garden of Harmony.

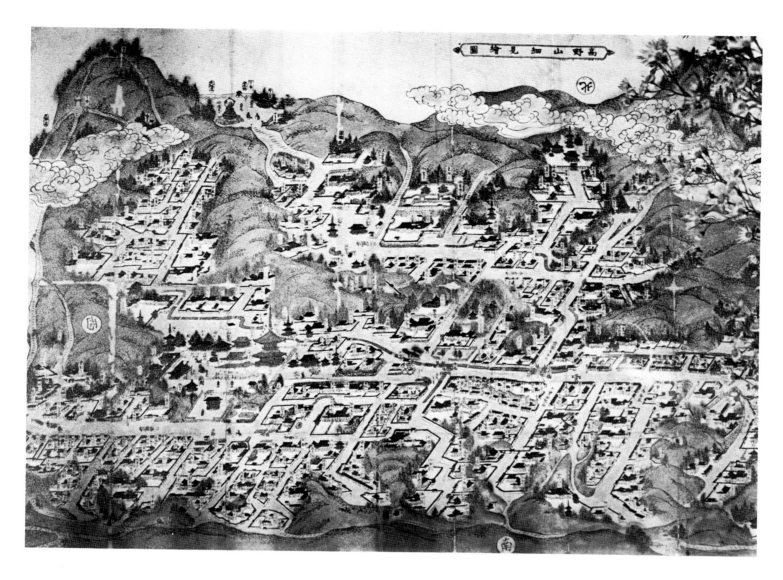

Anonymous: Bird's-eye view of the Mount Kōya monasteries (monastery of the Shingon sect of the Tentoku-in, Kōyasan). Detail of a kakemono.

Mount Kōya was chosen by the monk Kukai in the 9th century for the erection of temples and monasteries. It is dominated by eight peaks protecting it in the eight directions of space.

Kyōto: Garden of the Zuiho-in tea pavilion. Composition by Mirei Shigemori, 1938-1939.

While in China the top of a wall surrounding a garden is often marked by "dragon back" curves, in Japan it is always rectilinear. Dragon movements are suggested on the ground.

157

From Chang'an to Kyōto

In the year 645 Emperor Kōtoku came to the throne and decided that his country should adopt Chinese ways and Buddhism. He limited the construction of gigantic burial mounds and decreed that henceforth the bodies of the dead should be cremated; the money and energy saved would be used to build a fixed capital, Naniwa, on the site of the present Osaka. Having, unlike the Chinese, no experience of cities, he took as a model Chang'an, capital of the Tang dynasty.

It was a long time before the notion of a temporary capital disappeared. Between 656 and 794 (date of the foundation of Heian-kyō, which under the name of Kyōto remained the capital for more than a thousand years), and during the reigns of fourteen Emperors, thirteen imposing capitals were projected; some never came into being, the others, built at the cost of considerable effort, were then moved and rebuilt at great expense. Every time the model was still Chang'an, and the Fengshui rules were faithfully applied.

In the year 710 the Empress Gemmyō founded Heijo-kyō not far from the previous capital. The popular quarters were built in traditional style; lacking experience in the construction of buildings such as government offices, imperial palaces, princely mansions and Buddhist temples, the Japanese entrusted this work to architects and carpenters from the continent. At that time relations between China and Japan were good, although communications could be perilous.

In the year 742 two Japanese monks, members of a diplomatic mission, when on their way to the Tang capital met Jianzhen, superior of a recently created monastery at Yangzhou. They begged him to come and join them in Japan where, they told him, Buddhism was already well established but suffered from a shortage of "masters of discipline" of their standing. After five unsuccessful attempts to cross the sea, twelve years later, in 753, Jianzhen managed to land on Kyūshū Island. His favourite disciple had perished in a shipwreck and he himself had become blind. He finally arrived accompanied by painters, sculptors, jewellers, embroiderers, masons and masters of gardens; he also brought with him the Buddhist scriptures, relics, paintings and statues. Known in Japan as Ganjin, Jianzhen played a key role in bringing over the philosophy, culture and arts of the Tang dynasty. In 759, during a reconstruction of Heijo-kyō under the Emperor Seimu, a fervent Buddhist, Ganjin and his companions were asked to put up a Buddhist temple in the new capital. This edifice, the Tōshōdai-ji, is the only Tang style building that has survived intact until now.

The new style was generally approved, although it was the absolute contrary of the one that had preceded it, and of that which is still used for the construction of Shinto shrines. This can be seen by comparing it with the temples of Ise, which are destroyed and rebuilt in exactly the same form every twenty years, and are therefore true and unquestionable evidence of the traditional style of sixth century religious architecture in the islands. It was, however, accepted that the cult of a new religion of foreign origin should be celebrated in buildings of a style proper to it. Similarly, in 607 A.D., under the aegis of the Regent Shōtoku who introduced Buddhism from Korea, the Horyū-ji Temple was built by Korean artists in pure Korean style. The Tōshōdai-ji and the Horyū-ji, several times destroyed by fire and rebuilt, have kept their original appearance.

But what has become of the princely gardens of ancient Nara? Were they Korean, Chinese or Japanese in style? The garden, as we have said, is the most ephemeral of all arts, and there was little chance of finding again the stone compositions that had adorned the palaces of Heijo-kyō, the capital finally abandoned in 794 at the time of the foundation of Kyōto.

Portrait of the Monk Jianzhen (Ganjin). Dry lacquer with wooden support, overpainted in colours, a technique of southern China.

"This portrait admirably conveys the nobleness of Jianzhen, as mentioned in records of the period, and faithfully reproduces the peaceful figure of the blind old monk. The artist was probably one of his close friends, and the work must have been made shortly after the monk's death."

The stones of the prince

At the end of the seventeenth century, illustrating the *Tale of Genji* and recalling the mode for Chinese culture among aristocrats of the imperial court in Kyōto about the year 1000, Sumiyoshi Gukei (1631-1705) placed in the garden pool contemplated by the hero of the story, stone compositions representing the Isles of the Immortals similar to those of Chinese paintings and some Chinese gardens. In reality, no composition of the kind has been found in Japan. It cannot, however, be concluded that such compositions only existed in the imagination of the artist. Indeed, the fact that in the twelfth century the author of the *Sakutei-ki* had warned his contemporaries against the use of exceptional stones—"even brought from the mountain or river a stone with an exceptional appearance will become a divinity and cause many troubles"—warrants the assumption that the ten-

Sumiyoshi Gukei (1631-1705): Illustration of the *Tale of Genji* (*Genji monogatari*).

dency to use them was spreading. It seems that this stone style, the complete contrary of the one they were in the habit of using in the vicinity of their shrines in order to favour the descent of the *kami*, did not have the good fortune to please the Japanese. When they raised stones near their dwellings, the purpose they had in view was always to protect the home from harmful influences and attract and channel down heavenly energies, and they never used single stones as propagators of Breath Forces.

Whether or no Japanese masters did at one period raise stones in their gardens after the manner of the scholars' gardens in China is not very important since this passing fashion had no influence on the stone compositions constructed from the fourteenth century onwards in Zen monasteries, which are the oldest of such compositions to have come down to us.

161

Nara: Stone composition of the 8th century, discovered in 1976.

The stones of the seashore

The discussion concerning the genuinely native origin of Japanese stone compositions as opposed to their derivation from the gardens of the continent is still open. Some experts, including Mirei Shigemori, sought in their researches for evidence tending to prove that the art of raising stones, although influenced by Chinese culture, must have stemmed initially from the remotest prehistory of Japan. In this respect, the year 1976 was decisive; in that year the Nara Research Institute in one of its archaeological campaigns discovered a stone composition on the site of a palace dating from the time of the foundation of Heijo-kyō, in 710. Six feet below ground, the excavators unearthed rocks adorning the north bank of the pool. Professor Osamu Mori, who was directing the excavations, described this composition as "imposing." His enthusiasm was understandable. He had before him a typically Japanese composition, related to the stone arrangements set up in the vicinity of Shinto

shrines and forerunners of the studied compositions of the great fourteenth century Zen masters. Compositions of this kind are not found in China, but on the other hand, they illustrate perfectly the precepts of the *Sakutei-ki* as regards the size of the stones ("not more than five feet high"), their assembly ("once raised, one of them must predominate") and the direction of the axes, etc. Furthermore, in the part of the treatise dealing with the arrangement of the island, it is noted that in order to evoke a reef "you can put stones upright in some places and, according to the composition, add stones to represent the sea beating, the waves breaking. The stones should be sturdy, rough and rugged."

These compositions have little in common with the aesthetic effects sought in the Suzhou gardens through the use of stones from Lake Tai.

The *Sakutei-ki*, even if it only dates from the twelfth century, was not, in our view, written only

162

Uji, south of Kyōto: Garden of the Sambō-in, laid out by Hideyoshi from 1598 on.

as a means of adapting Chinese skills to Japanese conditions, but above all to safeguarding the very long-standing native tradition of evoking the Archipelago in stone compositions. It was essential that the ancestral rules should not be forgotten with the adoption of continental techniques. The Emperor might have placed the country under the protection of Buddha; the protection of the *kamis* must not cease on that account. This explains the author's insistence and repetitions when he considers the representation of coasts, islands—he describes ten kinds—and the sea: "If you want to represent the sea, first represent the shore... The stone arrangements should be virile. The combinations irregular, disorderly, rough, should express the shock of the waves, not only crashing on the beach but also on the high seas. Represent the big breakers, some reefs and peninsulas."

We know from writings of the Heian period that aristocrats liked to see an evocation of the sea in their garden pools. We even have a detailed description of a Kyōto garden where the pool was filled with sea-water. On the banks, servants burned seaweed, because in those days salt was extracted from seaweed by incineration and the sight of the smoke and the smell of the iodine reminded the prince of his walks along the beach.

In the paintings of the scholars as in their gardens, Chinese aesthetics had defined landscape (*shanshui*) giving priority to the term *shan*, or mountain, with *shui*, or water, the second term, setting off the value of the first. When Japanese aesthetics took over the Chinese definition of landscape, it made a slight change; the Mountain was no longer more important than its corollary Water (more riverine than maritime in China), but Water, implying the vision of the Sea with islands and reefs as a corollary, was the prior element abundantly expressed by artists in both landscape painting and gardens. The archaeological discovery at Nara only confirmed the intuition of the experts regarding the specifically Japanese origin of all the stone compositions connected with representations the Sea.

◁ △ Kyōto: Imperial Garden of the Silver Pavilion Temple (Ginkaku-ji).
Late 15th century.

Sign and form

Chinese symbolism made itself at home in the "Empire of Signs" without, however, ousting more ancient traditions. Traces of this cohabitation are everywhere to be seen; they are especially clear in these prints from the *Kyōto Garden Book* published in 1830.

The left-hand plate from the Kinkaku-ji Garden shows the ground for the reception of the *kami*. The entrance, marked by a portico, *torii*, leads to a covered platform where the ritual dances were performed to welcome the tutelary spirit come down from heaven to the altar placed on a little hill. The pond was dug in the Heian period, but the stone compositions in the middle of it were made later. They symbolize the mythical Isles of the Immortals, secured according to Chinese tradition on the back of giant turtles. The Japanese stone raisers kept the turtles, represented by the rocks breaking the surface of the water, evoking at the same time the islands and reflecting the influence of Chinese culture. Once again, however, the compositions on the banks portray various aspects of the coast of Japan.

The right-hand plate shows a stone composition entitled "Dragon Gate Waterfall," evincing again continental influence; there, too, the sign replaces the form.

Taking up again, in the mid-sixteenth century, the elements used by Chinese painters to illustrate the descent of the dragon, the artist Sōyū does not really paint a mountain, but an image of the mountain image depicted by the Chinese painters.

In portraying the Dragon Gate Waterfall, the artist leaves out the setting, present none the less by implication since the cascade could not have any other origin. All the attention of the spectator is therefore centred on the waterfall and the rock receiving it. At the same time, to suggest the height of the mountain, the artist has chosen from among the seven main types listed in the *Sakutei-ki*, the twin cascade (*mukai-ochi*), water falling down a breathtaking vertical rockface. [24] The left side, jutting out in clear-cut angular planes, is the sunny, predominantly Yang side; the one on the right, set back and in the shade, with a rounded summit, is predominantly Yin.

◁▷ Details.

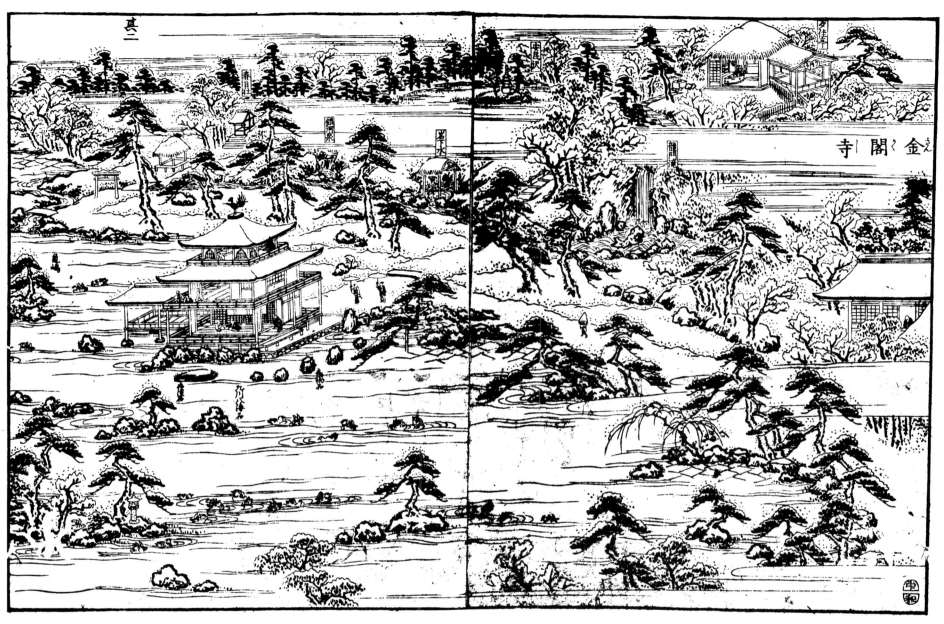

Two plates from the *Kyōto Garden Book*, 1830.
Garden of the Rokuon-ji, better known as the Kinkaku-ji (Golden Pavilion Temple).

The stone at the bottom of the waterfall is for all Japanese an image representing the carp swimming upstream, the carp which, legend has it, once at the top of the cascade will be transformed into a dragon. Here the fish-stone striving to reach the source of the torrent is the image of man in his desire to lose himself in the Whole. Indeed, the dynamic thrust of the rock makes it seem to be moving, while the water stays still. The engraver has given the rock a kind of appendix, a fish-tail, to make the resemblance complete. Just above the cascade, he has placed a bank of clouds to evoke the summits, as was often done in paintings at the level of the middle register.

167

168

◁ Sōyū (mid-16th century):
Poet Contemplating a Waterfall.
Japanese painting in the Chinese style.

▷ Kyōto: Garden of the Rokuon-ji.
Dragon Gate Waterfall.

Plate from Wang Gai's
Mustard Seed Garden Manual of Painting, 1679.

PAINTING BILLOWS

Mountains have strangely shaped peaks and water also has strangely shaped peaks. Rocks like great billows that roll and smash against mountains. When the moon is reflected on such waters, the waves are like galloping white horses, and at that moment one sees lofty mountains and peaks in their full grandeur.

Wang Gai.

THE WAY OF THE STONES

Mutō Shūi (14th century): Portrait of Musō Kokushi (1275-1351).
Silk scroll.

Yu Jian, Southern Song Dynasty: Mountains with Snowy Peaks. Painting of the Chan School.

Ongoing doctrines

The word Chan is a phonetical corruption of the Sanscrit concept Dyāna, to meditate or concentrate the mind. Chan was brought to China about 520 A.D. by the Indian Bodhidharma, who was then about sixty. Tradition relates that he attained the Awakening after having been nine years motionless meditating in front of a wall. Nine years was precisely the time needed to reach Perception of Tao by the method of internal alchemy developed by the Taoists.

Huike (487-593) was only accepted as his disciple and second Patriarch after he had cut off his arm to prove his determination. Since then, Chan teaching has been transmitted direct from master to disciples.

Up till the time of the third Patriarch, Shengcan (died c. 606), Chan adepts had no temples of their own; they led a wandering life, in close contact with the people on whose alms they depended for their subsistence. From the beginning, therefore,

Chan was imbued, more than the other Schools of Buddhism, with Chinese and Taoist ideas, as can be seen from these precepts taken from the third Patriarch's *Inscription on the Spirit of Faith*:

"Do not chase the world subject to causality,
Do not linger in emptiness excluding phenomena,
If you tear yourself away from the phenomenon,
it will engulf you.

If you pursue the void, you turn your back on it.
The more we talk and the more we speculate,
the further we go from the Way (Tao).
Rid of all speech and reflection, there is nowhere
we cannot go."

By the seventh century, Chan disciples, whose number grew rapidly, felt they should cover their needs by helping each other instead of troubling villagers by their begging. They founded monasteries far from towns and began to till the earth, seeking to attain the Awakening in and by a working life. That was why Chan was able to escape much of the persecution suffered between 842 and 845 by adepts of "foreign" religions, and stay longer in China.

For the Japanese, the foundation of the Chan School (Zen in Japanese) dates from the compilation of the first set of rules of conduct to be observed in a monastery, at the end of the eighth century. The School did not reach Japan until the last years of the twelfth century.

It was only in 1191 that the Japanese monk Eisai returning from China introduced, at the same time as the use of tea, the first Chan teachings, when he created the Rinzai Zen School (named after the Chinese monk Linzi, who died in 866). Thirty-six years later, Dōgen, another Japanese monk, who lived in China from 1123 to 1127, founded on his return the Soto School of Zen.

Contrary to the esoteric Buddhist Schools (Tendai, introduced by Saichō in 804, and Shingon, introduced by Kukai in 806, both of which advocated the Way of mandalas and rituals for the attainment of the Awakening), Zen claimed that the Awakening (in Japanese *satori*), the bursting of the bonds that bind us to our fixed mental structures, can and must be sustained and obtained by the sole means of mental concentration.

Sesshū Tōyō (1420-1506): Landscape in the Cursive Style (Haboku-sansui), 1495. Painting of the Zen School.

The Soto branch of Zen, preached by Dōgen, stressed the concept of *listening to the Universe*: "One must empty oneself and listen to the teaching of a real master, listen, listen, listen. Whether you understand or you don't understand, listen. Even in your sleep, because teaching penetrates by the pores of the skin."

173

Anonymous Chinese master (10th century): Landscape. Section of a scroll painting.

According to Chan doctrine, the study of texts is unnecessary, more likely than not to be harmful; instruction should be given direct, face to face by transmission of thought from mind to mind. Chan masters nevertheless left many writings, but these are mostly collections of speeches and poems, and not all-embracing systems of dogma. Their preferred means of expression were calligraphy and landscape painting. The Zen masters followed them in this, adding, from the fourteenth century onwards as a further means of transmitting their teaching, the stone compositions in their monasteries.

In 1342 the Japanese sent a ship to the continent. The profits made on the sale of the objects brought back were so great that they paid for the building at Kyōto of a new temple, the Tenryū-ji (Temple of the Celestial Dragon), which became the base of a branch of the Rinzai Zen sect. Subsequently, a regular sea link was maintained between this temple and China under the Yuan and Ming dynasties. The Zen monks from Kyōto who took part in these voyages were therefore often able to admire the stone compositions in the many monasteries at Yangzhou, the port where they landed.

Kyōto: Garden of the Tōfuku-ji Zen Monastery. Composition by Mirei Shigemori, 1938-1939.

The stone-bound instant

The ideogram *Mu:* Emptiness. Calligraphy by the Master Junyo Tanaka of the Shingon Buddhist School.

The oldest Zen stone compositions are attributed to the Tenryū-ji monks, in particular to the first abbot of the monastery, the poet Sōseki, great calligrapher and painter, better known by the name of Musō Kokushi. In 1339 he built for the Saihō-ji Temple at Kyōto (today called Kokedera or Moss Temple), dating from the Heian period, a stone composition which has never been restored and is the oldest example of this art practised by the Zen monks. This composition was intended to be the petrification of a moment, capturing the movement of the water not by the technique of ink on paper but by using one material to express another. The mountain whence the cascade surges forth is no longer even suggested, any more than the rock receiving the force of the falling water. We see nothing but the descent on earth of the Breath Force in a whirlpool of dry rocks seeming to burst out of the suddenly cleft ground in chaotic tumult suggesting silent thunder, a gaping wound, revealing the veins of the Dragon.

Like all the stone compositions created by the Zen masters, this one is an object lesson, a message that can be read on as many different levels of understanding as there are degrees of progress along the road to wisdom.

For some, this bounding cascade represents no more than the descent of the Breath Force; for others, it will be an image of the energy that can be set free by the un-doing of mental structures ossified by bad mental habits and made available for the unimpeded functioning of the mind; for others again, an image of the forces of passionate impulses they have to capture and harness so that no longer dominated by them, they can on the contrary make them serve with a view to the attainment of *satori*.

Kyōto: Garden of the Saihō-ji or Moss Temple (Kokedera).
Dry stone waterfall by Musō Kokushi, 1339.

177

Kōyasan: Stone composition at the entrance of the Sō-ji-in Monastery.

The stones of the Chan monasteries

Travelling from Peking to Suzhou, Emperor Qianlong put up at Buddhist monasteries some of which, refurbished for the occasion, are today derelict when they have not altogether disappeared. Pictures of all these posting-houses have been reproduced in a book entitled *Palaces of the Emperor six or seven leagues distant from each other along the road from Peking to Suzhou*. The illustrations show that in each of these monasteries there was at least one stone composition. These stones, drawn with the same precision as the architectural features of the buildings, were clearly "north stones," brownish with sharp ridges, expressive of an austerity more in keeping with monastic discipline than the elegance of the stones from Lake Tai. Two modes of expression existed side by side in China, the one favoured by the imperial court and scholars, the other reserved for the purposes of meditation and not found outside the precincts of the monasteries. When the Buddhist monks from Japan, such as

Ennin in the ninth century, Eisai at the end of the twelfth century, or Dōgen in the thirteenth century, went to China to complete their studies, staying in one monastery after another they were able to see and examine at leisure the stone compositions of the Chinese Buddhist masters. In view of the close relation between Japanese Zen paintings and those of the Chan masters of the Song period, such as Liang Kai (p. 182) or Yu Jian (p. 172), it can be assumed that the first compositions in Zen gardens were also inspired by those, today no longer extant, raised in Chan monasteries. The discovery of the ancient composition at Nara may, however, reopen the question of the solely Chinese sources for the inspiration of Zen artists; it might establish that, in order to convey their messages the Zen artists intuitively revived a more than six centuries old tradition, expression of a genuinely Japanese sensibility, which was to spread well beyond religious compositions to the gardens of lay persons.

Anonymous (18th century): One of the *Palaces of the Emperor*
along the road from Peking to Suzhou, six or seven leagues
from each other, detail.
The print is inscribed Xing gong long tan, *or halting-stage*
palace of the deep dragon lake.

Images
of the Universe

The author of the *Sakutei-ki* combined the Mountain of the Immortals with the Isles and at the end of his treatise, in the place usually kept in initiatory handbooks for important revelations, wrote as follows: "The Chinese generally put a spring near the dwelling and make a Horai mountain (Japanese for Mountain/Isles of the Immortals). According to Chinese tradition, a man who lives in this mountain never dies; Emperor Sui therefore gave the order to look for the mountain. According to Japanese tradition, the Mountain of Immortality is Japan." In this last message he adopted a somewhat condescending tone towards the powerful continental neighbours and their search for the Isles. He asserted that each mountain, each islet, each hillock of the Archipelago, inhabited by the *kami*, was a sacred place, a part of the Isles of the Immortals.

The giant turtles bearing the mythical islands on their backs were clearly related to the ancient Chinese cosmogony. Their hemispherical shell evoked the vault of heaven, their square ventral face represented the earth; it was the perfect square in a circle and circle in a square, the image of the Universe as symbolically portrayed in the complementary mandalas of the Diamond and the Matrix. From the fourteenth century onwards, Zen masters often took the turtle as a theme for their stone compositions; quit of the superposed Isle, the turtle was the image of Japan identified with the Universe, or more precisely with the Ultimate Reality of the Universe, not the Universe as it appears in its dualized form to men subject to relativity, but as it is perceived by one who has reached the Awakening. To the man who has reached this ultimate degree of awareness, the Ultimate Reality of the Universe appears as Void, Absolute, Uncreated. In this esoteric sense, the turtle, symbol of the Uncreated—therefore not subject to decay and death—becomes the symbol of Immortality.

The oldest stone composition in the form of a turtle to have survived unchanged was constructed

Kyōto: Garden of the Saihō-ji or Moss Temple.

by Musō Kokushi in 1339; it is also the most famous in Japan. "In the garden of the monk Musō, where centuries have passed," writes Kawabata in his novel *Sadness and Beauty*, "the stones had such an air of antiquity and acquired such patina that it was impossible to tell whether nature or the hand of man had set them in place..." This is so true that uninformed visitors to this Moss Garden pass close to the work of art without noticing it, although for Kawabata's heroine, a Japanese painter, "to see the rigid, angular forms of the stones, which weighed her down with an almost spiritual weight, there could be no doubt that it was a work of man." According to Mirei Shigemori, the moss surrounding the composition must have been the work of nature during a period when the garden was abandoned; he suggests that the original setting must have been white gravel. Today, the entire composition seems to float on an ocean of moss, each

rock, deeply rooted in the ground, breaks forth from a surging sea and braces itself to withstand the shock of the waves.

In his stone cascade, Musō Kokushi had expressed the flood of freed energies; here he shows the violence of the same energies, contained in a tense state of equilibrium. The forces of Yin and Yang often represented in China by the holes in stones, spaces necessary for movement, are, in accordance with specifically Japanese aesthetic rules, expressed by the intervals between the rocks.

Unlike most of the compositions constructed later and designed to be seen from a fixed point, Musō's turtle composition comes into view when rounding a small knoll in the course of the visit of the garden and is never seen as a whole; the infinite variety of viewpoints, the Multiple Whole, gives birth to the vision of its basic unity, the All in One.

For adepts of Zen, Awakening is attained sooner by humble and attentive contemplation of the world, even in its smallest and most matter of fact details, than by that of the mandalas. It may therefore seem surprising that the Awakened Musō Kokushi, in order to convey his mystical experience, should use themes so rich in symbolical values as the cascade or the crane. This should probably be seen as a typical aspect of Zen teaching, according to which the novice can only advance by constantly calling in question the operations of his mind.

Awakening, for the Zen adept, is only reached by the splintering of the mental structures that make the onlooker see a cascade or a turtle where there are only a few simple stones. Viewed in a state of complete receptivity, a stone composition, like any Object, only exists by virtue of the Subject contemplating it.

Attributed to Liang Kai, Song Dynasty: Ink Portrait of
an Immortal, c. 1250. Paper album leaf.

"The Ch'an painter's awareness of a single reality underlying the
seemingly disjunct phenomena of nature is communicated with the same
immediacy as the truths of the Ch'an doctrine, which cannot be
conveyed by translating them into the intellectual concepts of ordinary
discourse and expecting the listener to translate them back into
something like the original impulse. The Ch'an artist typically defines
his subject only at a few key points, leaving the rest ambiguous,
suggestive rather than descriptive. The viewer completes the image,
as the Ch'an novice pieces out by intuition the cryptic utterances
of the master."

James Cahill, *Chinese Painting*, 1960

PAINTINGS
TRANSPOSED

Kyōto, group of the Daitoku-ji Zen monasteries:
Ryōgen-in Garden.

The waterfall and the island

Musō Kokushi, first abbot of Tenryū-ji, would appear to have reduced the size of the already existing pond and composed, on the bank opposite the meditation hall, a waterfall which, at the time the *Kyōto Garden Book* was published (in 1830), was still fed by water pouring over rocks raised at successive levels.

The idea of this waterfall was taken from Song period pictures which the monks, from the first years of the thirteenth century, had brought back from China. Musō Kokushi was no doubt the first to introduce in Japan the three dimensional reproduction of Chinese landscape paintings in compositions to be seen from a fixed point.

Although Zen derives wholly from Chan and this waterfall wholly from Song painting, the garden is not on that account a transposition of Chinese gardens, according to what we know of them, including the drawings of the posting-houses of the Emperor Qianlong. There are original features precisely in the relation of the waterfall to the pond. The level water at the foot of the cascade which, through Chan, conveyed the essence of Taoist thought, as illustrated by Chinese painting, is neither the expression of a mountain lake, nor that of the calmed torrent, place for the concentration of the Breath Force, but owing to the presence of the island reef in the middle of the pond to the right of the cascade, an evocation of Japanese space. The pond is made to bear the image of the sea; in the *Taihei-ki*, a work relating the construction of Tenryū-ji, it is stated that "the rocks symbolize mountains in the fog," that "the plantations of trees reproduce the sound of the waves." The island, symbolizing the archipelago, is also there so that, while expressing the descent of the dragon, it recalls that the tutelary Shintoist *kami* need the mountain in order to be honoured by men and that a purified place is required for their descent.

These two major elements, the waterfall and the island, brought together by Musō Kokushi at Tenryū-ji, were to be the basic components of Zen gardens as these were constructed until the seventeenth century.

Anonymous Chinese master (10th century): Landscape. Section of a scroll.

Kyōto: Garden of the Celestial Dragon Monastery (Tenryū-ji).
The waterfall and the island, by Musō Kokushi, 1342.

The three planes of the landscape

The representation of the high mountain in painting is much more an exercise in style on a philosophical theme than a matter of precise reproduction of landscape. In order to embody it in the space of a garden, the Chinese artist often chose to make a high slope (p. 76) so that the privileged spectator, the person for whom the garden was designed or the one who built it, looking at it from a small pavilion, could see it in the same way as a painting, the upper third against the sky and the lower third reflected in the lake.

In the Garden of the Small Winding Valley at Yangzhou, the dragon rock raised thirty-three feet above the water could not be seen from more than forty-six feet away. The scholar, seated musing in his pavilion, could take in the whole of the garden

in his gaze, but had to raise or lower his head to study the details in the same way as he could if he were looking at a vertical picture.

Leaving the realm of the Chinese garden where a mountain-slope thirty-three feet high does not seem excessive in proportion to the immense size of the territory, we can only be struck by the diametrically opposed way of expressing the mountain in the Japanese garden. Not, as might be thought, that the stone compositions were going to be "shrunk" proportionately to Japanese consciousness of the diminutive size of their archipelago but, this being only a mountainous arc, the nearness of the heights made it unnecessary to express them; it was enough to represent their quintessence.

From the meditation hall 130 feet away, a spectator could see the sixteen foot high waterfall at Tenryū-ji in its entirety without having to move or even to raise or lower his eyes. Fixing his gaze on the waterfall, he could take in all its details while with his peripheric vision seeing the pond below and the Arashiyama hill above.

The space given to Gardens of Longevity was always commensurate with the means of their owners, and there were many gardens of modest proportions in China that have disappeared. In Japan, and particularly at Kyōto, throughout the fourteenth and fifteenth centuries, many Rinzai School monasteries were built, chiefly in the big complexes at Myōshin-ji to the west and Daitoku-ji to the north of the capital, the latter comprising thirty-three small monasteries grouped around the central temple. The space assigned to each of the monasteries was limited and the Zen monks were forced to plan very small meditation gardens. This led them to bring the waterfall in their composition closer to the observation point, reducing its height according to the distance from which it would be seen. In this way, a composition not more than five and a half feet high, seen from thirty-three feet away, could give the same kind of view as the Tenryū-ji waterfall.

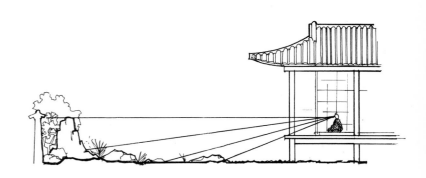

It is a moot point whether the Kyōto gardens, so famous that thousands of tourists visit them every day, can convey to momentary onlookers the message of their creators, but there still exist more discreet gardens where the visitor, squatting at the centre of the podium surrounding the meditation hall, can analyse in silence and solitude the method used by the Zen monks to transpose in three dimensions the landscapes of Chinese painting.

Kyōto, Temple of the Nishi Hongan-ji: Kokei Garden evoking a famous Chinese landscape.

The Wang Fu painting entitled *Literary Meeting in a Mountain Lodge* is typical of literati paintings of the Ming period. It includes the classical themes of the cascade, the descent of the dragon, distant mountains and the division of the composition in three registers. If we compare this with the stone composition constructed by the painter Kanō Motonobu, we notice that the space in the Chinese painting has been reproduced by a flat projection of the lower two-thirds of the composition, the uppermost third alone being evoked by the raised stones. This method, repeated in many gardens, makes it possible on the one hand to use only small stones, following the old tradition "not more than five feet high," and on the other hand, to bring the spectator into direct contact with the composition as if he were himself one of the personages usually appearing in the lowest third of paintings.

In drawing a parallel between a given Japanese stone composition and a given Chinese painting, we are not trying in any way to prove that the Japanese artist had this same picture before him. The sole purpose of comparing Japanese stone compositions with Chinese paintings is to illustrate the transposition techniques used by the Japanese artists and their astonishing fidelity to the pictorial conventions established by the Chinese scholars in respect of both form and composition.

"The divisions, when they are made according to the method of three successive planes, or two sections," Shitao writes in his *Remarks on Painting* (Ch. 10), "seem doomed to make a hash of landscape; the only divisions that are not harmful are those traced by Nature herself... If each landscape is to be the subject of a kind of decoding and cut into pieces, the result cannot possibly be anything living since the eye will see at once that it has been manufactured.

"The division in three planes consists in a foreground for the ground, a second plane for the trees and a third for the mountain. But in front of that, how can the spectator have any feeling of depth? If this method of three planes is used, how can the painting produced be any different from an engraved plate?

Kyōto, group of the Myōshin-ji Zen monasteries: Taizo-in Garden attributed to the painter Kanō Motonobu (1476-1559).

Anonymous Chinese
master, Yuan Dynasty:
Autumn Colours by
a Fishing Village.
Silk scroll.

189

山亭雅會

永樂甲申中穐日九龍山
人王孟端畫

縱橫峯軸與雲神勝
家畫田六七人印譜
恰枝行蓬畫重君己
卯仲之春

峯若抽簪瀑
醉紳樓逆于
野會同人呼
之欲出鮮葉
蒚古勘梁溪
己卯仲春
尚題

Wang Fu (1362–1416), Ming Dynasty: Literary Meeting in a Mountain Lodge. Paper scroll.

Kyōto, group of Myōshin-ji Zen monasteries: Taizo-in Garden.

"The division in two sections consists in placing the scene at the bottom and the mountain at the top and adding some conventional clouds in between to separate the two sections more clearly.

"What is needed, in reality, is that the same breath of inspiration should run through the three elements of the composition. Do not let yourself be kept in chains by these pedantic conventions of three planes and two sections. On the contrary, attack vigorously, so that all the force of your brush strokes can be seen; then, even if you get involved in a succession of a thousand summits and ten thousand valleys, there will be no trace of vulgarity in your painting as a whole.

"Once inspiration is indwelling in the three elements of the composition, even if there is still weakness here and there in details, these will do no harm to the whole."

After having quoted Shitao, one wonders whether it is still possible to make a relatively descriptive analysis of a Chinese painting without seeming to engage in sterile dissection. We do not think, however, that Leng Qian falls in the category of the laborious workers who let themselves be enchained in "these pedantic conventions" of certain later painters to whom Shitao referred. This Leng Qian landscape corresponds perfectly to the divisions noted by the Monk Bitter Pumpkin; it will suffice to indicate a few details, starting from the bottom of the composition. The bottom register shows a stretch of calm water, the tumultuous currents come down from the heights passing through the central register, where luxuriant wild greenery fed by clouds and condensation is dotted here and there with the houses of simple foresters or solitary sages; in the top register, the treatment of the summits plainly expresses the living structure of matter and, more than its veins, the chine of the single dragon. In the bottom register again, beyond the bridge, a rock repeats unmistakably the form of one of the summits.

To interpret correctly the parallel between this landscape and the Daisen-in waterfall (p. 193), it will be necessary to take away the tall rock to the left which, separated from the waterfall group by a small space, belongs to a neighbouring composition, or more correctly includes this group in a second theme which will be considered later (p. 200).

The garden waterfall, whether the water is real or, as here, represented by gravel, is both in design and in execution a Japanese creation, although directly inspired by Chinese landscape paintings. The Daisen-in composition is indeed one of the most faithful transcriptions of the message conveyed by the Chinese waterfall; it embodies a profound and important Taoist theme, the descent of the Breath Force and its radiation over men and things. The creator of the Daisen-in waterfall, no longer treating the landscape in three, but in two registers, has

Attributed to Leng Qian (c. 1310-1371), Ming Dynasty: Mount Boyue or Jinhuashan (Anhui). Silk scroll.

191

kept only the essential features: in the foreground, the arrival of the life forces in the form of the torrent slowed down by the stones below the bridge; then, at the foot of the summits, the basin of run-off waters. All the stones, raised or just breaking the surface of the gravel, have been chosen so that their shape and structure should evoke the Veins of the Dragon.

To understand the approach of these creators, it has to be remembered that for Zen monks stone compositions had an educational aim. They were required to retransmit the teaching of the Chan masters, and this teaching could only be communicated from mind to mind or by the intermediary of an inspired work of art.

It has been shown in the Chinese part that landscape painting and the stone compositions of the Gardens of Longevity, based on component principles of the cosmic vision of the Middle Empire and the Fengshui rules, had nevertheless been expressed in divergent forms; the garden was not really the three-dimensional reproduction of a landscape painting. Our insistence, when deciphering the Japanese garden, in continuing to refer to Chinese rather than Japanese painting might pose a problem for the reader. In the periods prior to the Zen gardens the Japanese, adopting the technique of ink and brush, already owed everything to China. In their calligraphy, the Zen monks were directly inspired, often at several centuries distance, by that of the Chan masters, whose meditation techniques they wished to take over and continue. In painting, they copied the techniques of the Chinese and often their landscapes, even if they gave preference to Buddhist themes and included typical views of the archipelago. For the creation of their gardens, however, they did not go to their own painting for inspiration. For their stone compositions, absolutely original compared with those of their continental counterparts, they drew their inspiration direct from the great Chinese painters who had so amply conveyed in their works the great cosmic breath of their philosophy. So as not to distort the inexpressible message, they set themselves to transpose as faithfully as possible these initiatory paintings in the meditation gardens of their monasteries, absolute fidelity to the original models being indispensable for the maintenance of the esoteric content of the teaching.

Fang Congyi, Yuan and early Ming Dynasty: Immortal Mountains and Numinous Woods. Paper scroll.

Kyōto, group of Daitoku-ji Zen monasteries: Dry stone waterfall
of the Daisen-in Monastery, attributed to Sōami, 1509.

Plate from the *Kyōto Garden Book* showing the Reiun-in Garden
of the group of Daitoku-ji Zen monasteries, 1830.

The Zen monk Lu Tong, as he prepares tea, faces his guest, who is seated with his back to the stones of a transposed painting, in the radiance of the Garden of Longevity. Lu Tong too steeps himself in the Breath Force, but the artist has represented him turning away from an elaborate composition. He thus illustrates the story of Lu Tong declining the social ascension symbolized by the rock and the banana tree.

Two images proposed for the tea ceremony practised by the Tang and the Song, and taken over by the Zen monks from the fifteenth century on. As he watches the toads salute the autumn rain, Lu Tong, the accomplished scholar of the Tang dynasty, sings of tea: "The first cup wets my lip and throat, the second breaks my solitude, the third penetrates my flesh and blood and stirs up thousands of strange ideograms, the fourth gives me a slight perspiration, and all the badness of my life runs out through my pores; with the fifth cup, I am purified; the sixth carries me into the realm of the Immortals. And the seventh! Ah! the seventh... But I can drink no more than that! I feel the breath of the cold wind puffing out my sleeves. Where are the Mountains of the Immortals? Ah, let me be carried thither on the wings of that soft breeze!"

ART AND LONGEVITY

Attributed to Qian Xuan, Song Dynasty:
Lu Tong Brewing Tea.
Paper scroll.

195

Chinese philosophy, Japanese perception

The Daisen-in garden, created in 1509, extends in a north-east-south arc. The waterfall (p. 193) placed to the north-east protects the buildings from harmful influences from that direction, a protection strengthened by the presence on the left of a three-stone composition, the *san zon seki* or Stones of the Three Saints.

On the one side and the other, the familiar turtle and crane compositions are found to the left and right of the waterfall respectively, representing Japan allegorically as the Isle of the Immortals. The whole forms a horseshoe-shaped protective barrier in conformity with the Fengshui rules. The energies of the Breath Force, descending from the mountain, are slowed down by the rock blocks arranged at the foot of the waterfall. The stone to the left of the bridge evokes very realistically the violence of the water beating on the stones and the boom of breaking waves. Below the bridge there is a calmer zone. The monastery thus appears to be

Kyōto, first part of the Daisen-in Garden:
The Crane.

196

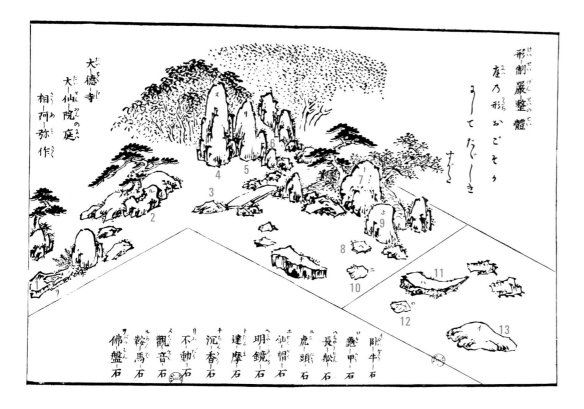

Kyōto: Plan of the Daisen-in.
Plate from Volume III of
the *Tsukiyama Niwatsukushi no den*
(Building Tradition of
Artificial Mountains and Gardens)
by Sigeyoshi, 1735.

1 Buddha's footprint
2 Turtle island
3 Stone splashes
4 Kannon stone
5 Fudō stone
6 Waterfall
7 Daruma stone
8 Bright mirror stone
9 Hermit's head stone
10 Tiger's head stone
11 Treasure boat
12 Turtle stone
13 Sleeping buffalo stone

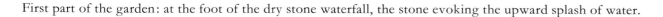

First part of the garden: at the foot of the dry stone waterfall, the stone evoking the upward splash of water.

Kyōto, second part of the Daisen-in Garden: left, the Treasure Boat stone; right, the Mount Hiei stone (Eisanseki).

located in its entirety in a Dragon's Lair, enabling the monks to benefit from the regenerating impact of the Breath Force.

The plan published in 1735 shows the north-east corner of the garden. To the right, a simple line indicates the narrow covered footbridge separating the first part of the garden from the next. The second garden flows, in every sense of the word, from the first. Its theme, quite rare in the gardens that survive, is that of the smoothly flowing river, undulating like a dragon, the Dragon of the East, whose veins follow the traces of a rake on the white gravel. To the left, a recumbent stone in the form of a ship drifts slowly past a landscape of mountains

and hills standing out against the white sky of the surrounding wall. The treatment of the whole is like that of a *makemono* (painted or written scroll to be unrolled horizontally) intended to be contemplated slowly. The distance to be covered by the eyes from left to right as far as the end of the reach is as short as the life of a man.

After the last lock, the Breath Force inclines to the west to flow into a sea represented by a stretch of white gravel; there, at a slightly lower level, is the third part, the South Garden. The monastery is therefore wholly in the *dragon's belly*.

Part of the message of the creator of the Daisen-in appears in this South Garden in the form of two gravel mounds. It would be hazardous and vain to seek for a single explanation. The dragon cycle was continuous and it is reasonable to see, in these two mounds pointing skywards, the suggested ascending movement of forces embodied in the Bounding Dragon taking off at the beginning of his celestial flight, in the form of clouds, prior to his return to earth on the mountain tops. In a Shinto context, these two mounds could be interpreted in the light of the two cones of white sand raised in the Shimogamo shrine at Kyōto on the occasion of certain festivals (p. 154) when they illustrate the legend of the creation of Japan: "At that moment, the salt drops that fell from the halberd, superposed, became Islands," runs the *Kojiki*. We have described the waterfall as an example of the transposition of a landscape painting (p. 185); here, we are considering the garden as an attempt at the harmonization of Chinese philosophical ideas and Japanese perception of a Universe in which a certain aesthetic sensibility is brought into play.

In connection with Zen monasteries, it is important always to remember that the aim of Buddhism is to overcome death by breaking the cycle of rebirths. In this setting, we can take it that the presence of these two mounds of gravel is also related to the concept of Awakening and Immortality. Thus, by its situation following the part of the garden illustrating human life, this third part of the garden refers us back to the first inhabitants of *dai sen*, "Great Immortals" for whom the Universe is no longer perceived in dualized form.

Kyōto, third part of the Daisen-in Garden.

Three, five, seven stones

大德寺
方丈

Kyōto, Daitoku-ji Zen monasteries: North-west corner of the Garden of the Mother House (Hōjō). Plate from the *Kyōto Garden Book*, 1830.
View at the present time, with details on p. 201.

In the meditation garden of the *hōjō*, mother house of the Daitoku-ji, to the north-west of the abbot's residence there are three raised stones also evoking a waterfall. Initially, and this can still be seen in the plates of the *Kyōto Garden Book*, the composition was so arranged that the Arashiyama hill in the distance served as a background, in accordance with the *borrowed landscape* technique. Here, however, as at Tenryū-ji, shrubs have been left to grow so high that the composition has been shorn of its top register. The descent of the Breath Force, originally channelled from the distant background summits down to the foot of the waterfall, passing by the raised stones, can no longer be followed. The waterfall has become the principal if not the only register of a composition which differs slightly from other representations of waterfalls in so far as the reference to landscape painting is much less in evidence.

In the photograph of the Daisen-in mineral waterfall there appeared to the left a raised stone belonging to a neighbouring composition called *san zon seki*, or Stones of the Three Saints, placed so close to the first that a spectator off his guard might think it was part of the waterfall. The Three Saints group is found in many Japanese gardens; its origin, quite old and not very clear, seems to be the result of the merging and assimilation of several concepts among which it is possible to discern that of the Tao as expressed in one of the definitions of Laozi: "The Tao begets the One, the One begets Two, Two begets Three, Three begets the infinity of creatures."

Buddhist mythology, more than philosophy, uses this Three to represent the *self in three bodies*; the Three Saints groups are always raised stones, relatively tall and arranged side by side on the same axis, and their role is also to channel the supernatural forces of the Japanese cosmic universe, that is to say to favour the descent of the tutelary spirits. The *Sakutei-ki*, in the chapter on waterfalls, states: "Fudo Miyo [pseudonym of a Master of Gardens in the Heian period] has told us that *waterfalls are also the image of the Three Saints*." This superimposition of meanings is the key to the interpretation of this waterfall composed of three raised stones.

Since the engraver has depicted the north-west corner of the garden seen from above with part of the roof of the meditation hall in the foreground, to the right of the waterfall there appears a stone composition with a crane and turtle facing each other. The stone groups on the left side of the garden, along the clipped hedge, deserve special attention on account of the messages they convey. It should be noted that their north-south orientation places them in line with the currents descended from the distant mountains (therefore beyond the corner of the surrounding wall) and collected by the waterfall. The height of these groups diminishes progressively with their distance from the waterfall, like so many heaps of scree borne there by the current. Each one is composed of a raised stone together with stones laid on the ground (sometimes also a small round trimmed bush having the same meaning).

For this type of stone garden composition, the author of the *Sakutei-ki* prescribes: "When the stones are arranged, one of them should predominate. In this there is a secret: the stones should form a slope. The water of the river beats against the stones and changes direction; each of the stones should be sturdy enough to withstand the current. As the force of the current gradually diminishes, this diminution must be expressed, creating a slight aesthetic impression."

This text is again an analogy with the representation of the streams flowing down the mountainside by stages as shown in Chinese landscape paintings.

The stones raised against the current they regulate, at the same time imbibing its beneficent exhalations and passing them on to the recumbent stones, were chosen for the quality of their summit and their apt expression of the Veins of the Dragon. We have described these compositions in the first place as rocks, portions of mountain drained by streams, but it is impossible not to see in them also the groups of three, five or seven stones—series of uneven numbers being considered lucky in Japan —arranged to represent the Japanese archipelago thrown up by the formidable thrust of the marine deep. Thus only the top of these stones, deeply anchored in the soil, emerges from the ground. Furthermore, the islands of the archipelago are called to mind even more forcefully by the beaches of moss surrounding each composition. They

seem, it is true, to be drawn out in the direction of the current, but at the same time they reproduce the typical lengthwise extension of the China Sea. In common with the stones excavated at Nara (p. 162), they have a specifically Japanese aspect.

The theme of the islands was widely developed, particularly in Zen gardens. It can be considered to have reached its apogee in the stone compositions in the Ryōan-ji garden which are in every respect an expression of Japan in terms of space. They seem, however, to have much greater fascination for foreign travellers than for Japanese researchers.

Undoubtedly the most famous garden in Japan, the Ryōan-ji is officially attributed to Sōami, who lived in the late fifteenth and early sixteenth century.

Once a renowned Zen master had stayed in a monastery, later historians were only too ready to credit him with having created all the masterpieces of the locality. It might seem preferable that the name of the creator of a work of genius should be unknown. It seems that the chronicle forgot that of the obscure artist who composed the stone garden at Ryōan-ji.

The attribution to Sōami gives, however, food for thought, for there is no mention of this garden in any text earlier than the seventeenth century. On the other hand, in the Hideyoshi period the monastery precincts included a garden with a pond, which was famous for its cherry trees admired by many people who came to see them when they were in flower. This garden still exists, but is hardly ever visited.

The Ryōan-ji stone garden belongs to the three-five-seven type, that is to say it comprises three groups of stones composed of

three stones,
three stones plus two stones,
five stones plus two stones.

This was a classical type of garden of the Momoyama period (1573-1603). It falls in the category of mineral gardens, abstract exercises of Zen monks. It seems, moreover, to be their supreme achievement in this genre.

This composition appears also to have been influenced by the *bon seki* or pebble arrangements on a tray covered with sand, a refined diversion of seventeenth century aesthetes consisting in the arrangement of a few pebbles on a horizontal plane in accord with a specific harmony and following the rules for the arrangement of stones in gardens.

Thus the *bon seki* were inspired by the gardens and the Ryōan-ji reproduced a *bon seki* on garden scale. The cycle was complete. After this last exercise in style, the garden masters had to look for another form of expression.

Rather than an avant-garde work, the Ryōan-ji garden seems to us to be the final and perfect culmination marking the end of a period.

"At the Ryōan-ji in Kyōto, whatever the point of view adopted, the fifteen stones can be seen, all except one. Have we here the mystical experience of a Zen Buddhist monastery? Or does all mystique consist in eliciting a theme from the silence inherent in the meaning, in which every indicator is, by degrees, the expounder of others, and in which there is never any final expounder nor any final expounding."
Henri Van Lier, *L'animal signé*, 1980.

Plate from a book by Suzuki Harunobu (1725-1770).

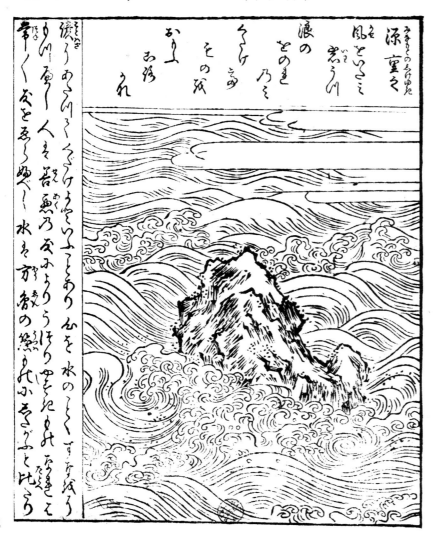

202

Kyōto, Garden of the Ryōan-ji Zen Monastery.

The message of the Gardens of Longevity

"Therefore, what is called *art*, since it calms the minds of all, and moves the great and the lowly, might be a first step towards increased longevity and happiness, a means of prolonging life."

The great Japanese playwright Zeami (1365-1443) is the probable author of this definition, one of the most brilliant that has been given of art, although he put it forward in the *Secret Tradition of Nō*[25] as taken from the (hypothetical) book of *Secrets*. He had written it for the benefit of actors. In Japan, as in other civilizations, the theatre, stemming from ancient religious origins, had in the course of time lost its contact with religion and become a profane entertainment. By his treatise Zeami restored drama to a higher level. In choosing to quote him, besides the beauty of the text, we invoke directly the link between the stone raiser and the actor; the one and the other tend in their creations to un-realize the real and realize the un-real, which is precisely to practise an art.

The Fengshui rules in China had defined the best structures for the ideal residence; other rules, similar or distinct, had imposed constraints in Japan. The creators of Gardens of Longevity, anonymous or famous artists, had worked to these rules. Through the *Sakutei-ki*, we have discovered the basic aims of the Japanese garden; we take these up again by way of conclusion because they seem to us so clearly perceptible also in the compositions of Chinese gardens.

Symbolic re-creation of an ideal environment in which man can take his place and live happily.

The symbolic re-creation of an ideal environment: what man from the Mediterranean basin, cradle of Judeo-Christian civilizations, themselves issued from earlier civilizations, has not dreamed of a garden reflecting a fancied or materialized Eden?

This first aim must therefore be considered to belong to Homo Universalis.

To be a vision of the "Pure Land" of Buddha Amida, of the Cosmic Unity of the one who reaches Awakening.

In the twelfth century, at the time the *Sakutei-ki* was compiled, Amidism was in favour at the imperial court in Kyōto. According to this doctrine of salvation, the Awakening could not be obtained during earthly existence; the followers of Buddha Amida entered the Paradise of the "Pure Earth" after death. Hence the custom at this time, towards the end of the Heian period, of constructing to the south of residences gardens reproducing Chinese prints of the "Western Paradise." In this, Japan was perhaps following, at a certain distance, a vision that had already faded in China, where the scholar's garden expressed earlier, still living themes stemming from the cosmic vision of Taoist philosophy.

To enable man, through meditation, to advance along the way of spiritual search leading to Awakening.

In twelfth century Japan, while believers in the Paradise of Amida extolled the Pure Earth, esoteric Buddhism of the Tendai and Shingon Schools taught the notion of Awakening obtained during life on earth developed by the Zen who, setting aside meditation on symbolic representations of the Cosmos (mandalas), gave more importance to stones as a means of attaining to Awakening. Monastic meditation, as we can assume this to have been practised in the Chan monasteries of China, upheld the contemplative attitude to nature of the very first Buddhists and above all of the Taoist masters. The scholar, leading a secular life by definition, used this as a means of escaping social constraints and seeking Awakening in both the Buddhist and the Taoist meaning of the term.

Suzhou: Garden to Linger In.

To facilitate the descent of the tutelary spirits.

A focal point of life forces in China, the stone is a mountain or part of a mountain, a sign representing the Veins of the Dragon, or the race of the clouds. In the imperial gardens it remains the primordial mountain, the link between Heaven and Earth. A focal point of the landscape in Japan, the stone is the substitute for the mountain, vested with the same powers as the mountain for the reception of tutelary spirits (the *kami*) descending towards men in order to regenerate them in accordance with a native tradition predating the influence of Chinese culture.

To be a micro-image of Japan identified with the Isles of the Immortals of Chinese tradition.

This moving reminder of an identity to be preserved reflected certain rules of conduct. During many centuries, foreign influences were never powerful enough in China to weaken a very strongly structured civilization; in Japan at all periods, some particularly watchful minds feared lest the impact of foreign knowledge obliterate the old traditions.

To stimulate aesthetic feeling by the re-creation of a space [Japan peopled by divinities] where a cult of beauty could be celebrated.

The placing of the insular reference in brackets gives this final aim the universal value expressed by the first, and provides a definition appropriate to both China and Japan of the space occupied by the raised stones, which we have called "Garden of Longevity." The Chinese were the oldest and the greatest theoretical masters of painting. Jing Hao, a solitary painter who lived during the first half of the tenth century, wrote a treatise, the *Bifa Ji*, which according to Pierre Ryckmans is one of the peaks of Chinese aesthetic thought. He was the first to "deduce a set of logical conclusions making it possible to found an authentic system of aesthetics. The ultimate aim of painting is not *decorative beauty* but *truth*. What is *truth*? It must not be confused

◁▷ Yangzhou: Garden of the Shi Kefa Memorial Temple (Shigongci).
Stone compositions on either side of a circular opening.

Shi Kefa was a late Ming official at Yangzhou. When the Qing took power, he refused to submit and attempted suicide. He was finally arrested and executed. His body was never recovered, but in the tomb erected for him his clothes were buried and a temple, the Shigongci, surrounded by a garden, was dedicated to him.

Peking, Forbidden City: Palace of Tranquil Longevity
before the entrance of the Pavilion of Expected Luck.

with *formal resemblance*; indeed, formal resemblance only reaches the appearance of things, whereas the function of truth is to capture their essence." [26] To the *Six Rules of Painting* of Xie He (c. 500 A.D.) Jing Hao added new notions "so as to see painting only from the universal standpoint of its threefold essence: spiritual (Breath, Rhythm, Thought), natural (the natural scene) and plastic (Brush and Ink)." [27] Brush and Ink were replaced by the creators of the Gardens of Longevity by Stone (or the texture of Stone) and the arrangement of Stone in Space.

The components of the Garden of Longevity are stones. The West, discovering those of Japan some decades ago, appreciated them for their severity which was in keeping with the rejection of the flam-boyant style and superfluous decoration in vogue at that time. The meaning of the stones is perhaps less immediately noticeable in Chinese Gardens of Longevity owing to the proliferation of more complex signs to be deciphered; also, they generally have to be interpreted in a more narrative manner. As far as our knowledge allowed, we have tried to read their meaning, and have sought to understand why the Way of Stones spread so widely in Japan but not in any other country that came into contact with China.

Tao is innumerable. Artists have used the Way of Stones as they used the Way of the Brush. Using his own way the dramatist Zeami wrote on art, and his definition applies to all Ways capable of conveying to humanity the so fragile message of Beauty, that is to say of Wisdom.

Kyōto, group of the Daitoku-ji Zen monasteries: Ryōgen-in Garden.

DEDICATION

The restoration of diplomatic relations between present-day China and Japan was long and laborious; initiated by the latter, it reached a successful conclusion in the 1970s. The Japanese government then offered to build a replica of the Tōshōdai-ji, which the monk Jianzhen had erected at Nara in 759. In 1976 a team of Japanese specialists went to Yangzhou to begin the work in the precincts of the Daming temple, of which the doctor-monk had been one-time Superior. This gesture was the tribute of a people in the front rank of modern industrial techniques who, far from disowning their past, had not forgotten Jianzhen, who had brought them the famous Tang culture. Still more moving was the gesture of the anonymous stone raisers who, their contract completed, went to the square before the west door of the Temple to compose a few stones to the memory of the great master, and re-establish in their way the communication, by means of conventions, signs and codes, between two peoples drawn together by the signs conveyed by stones as by their ideographic writing.

NOTES

[1] Shitao, *Remarks on Painting by the Monk Bitter Pumpkin*. References are to Shitao, *Les Propos sur la peinture du moine Citrouille-amère*, French translation and commentary by Pierre Ryckmans, Hermann, Paris 1984, p. 131.

[2] *Ibid.*, p. 102.

[3] *Ibid.*, p. 107.

[4] Léon Hoa, *Reconstruire la Chine, trente ans d'urbanisme, 1949-1979*, Editions du Moniteur, Paris 1981, p. 216.

[5] Shitao, *Les Propos*, p. 89.

[6] *Ibid.*, p. 73.

[7] *Ibid.*, p. 10.

[8] *Ibid.*, p. 23.

[9] Chen Congzhou, *On Chinese Gardens*, Tongji University Press, Shanghai 1985, pp. 22, 51.

[10] Marcel Granet, *Fêtes et chansons anciennes de la Chine*, Albin Michel, Paris 1982, p. 177.

[11] Shen Fu, *Six Stories as the Fickle Days Go By*. Reference is to Shen Fu, *Six récits au fil inconstant des jours*, French translation from the Chinese by Pierre Ryckmans, Christian Bourgeois Editeur, Paris 1982, p. 202.

[12] *Ibid.*, pp. 197-198.

[13] James Cahill, *Chinese Painting*, Skira, Geneva–London–New York 1960, new edition 1977, p. 26.

[14] D. and V. Elisseeff, *La civilisation de la Chine classique*, Arthaud, Paris 1981, pp. 252-253.

[15] James Cahill, *Chinese Painting*, p. 26.

[16] Pierre Seghers, *Sagesse et poésie chinoises*, French translation by Marie-Thérèse Lambert, Robert Laffont Editeur, Paris 1981, p. 36.

[17] Hubert Damisch, *Théorie du nuage, pour une histoire de la peinture*, Seuil, Paris 1972, pp. 279-280.

[18] Shitao, *Les Propos*, Annexe V, p. 217.

[19] *Ibid.*, p. 101.

[20] Shen Fu, *Six récits*, p. 142.

[21] Joseph Needham, *Science and Civilisation in China*, Cambridge University Press, 1954.

[22] Fritjof Capra, *Le Tao de la physique*, Tchou, Paris 1979, p. 246.

[23] Professor Narimitsu Matsudaira, "Le rituel des prémices au Japon," in *Bulletin de la Maison Franco-Japonaise*, new series, IV, 2, 1955, Tokyo 1957.

[24] Pierre and Susanne Rambach, *Sakutei-ki ou Le Livre secret des Jardins japonais*, complete translation into French of an unpublished Japanese manuscript of the late twelfth century, Skira, Geneva 1973, p. 138.

[25] Zeami, *The Secret Tradition of Nō*. Reference is to Zeami, *La tradition secrète du Nô*, French translation by René Sieffert, Gallimard, Paris 1960, p. 98.

[26] Shitao, *Les Propos*, p. 229.

[27] *Ibid.*, p. 227.

LIST OF GARDENS
BIBLIOGRAPHY
LIST OF ILLUSTRATIONS
INDEX
ACKNOWLEDGMENTS

LIST OF GARDENS

WITH STONE COMPOSITIONS ILLUSTRATED IN THIS BOOK

CHINA

Peking

FORBIDDEN CITY:

- GARDEN OF THE PALACE OF TRANQUIL LONGEVITY (NINGSHOUGONG), at the north-east corner of the Forbidden City. First erected in 1689, the palace was rebuilt in 1772-1776 by the Emperor Qianlong, who wished to retire there after his abdication. Now being restored, this garden was not yet open to the public in 1985.
- IMPERIAL GARDEN (YUHUAYUAN), in the centre of the north side of the Forbidden City. It was laid out under the Ming and some of the trees are said to date from that time.
- COURTYARD OF THE PALACE OF INHERITING HEAVEN (XUANQIONG).

ZHONGSHAN PARK, a site once occupied by the Temple of the Country's Rebirth (Xingguosi). Here in 1421 a Ming emperor set up the Altar of the Soil and Harvests (Shejitan). In 1914 it became a public garden. In 1928 it was named Zhongshan Park in memory of Dr. Sun Yat-sen (known to the Chinese as Sun Zhongshan). Several pavilions and stone compositions were then moved here from other gardens (in particular from the Yuanmingyuan).

BEIHAI PARK:

- GARDEN OF SERENITY STUDY (JINGXINZHAI), on the north shore of Lake Beihai. Built in 1757 in the reign of the Emperor Qianlong. This restored garden is now open to the public, except for the south-western part.
- GARDEN OF THE PAINTED BOAT RETREAT (HUAFANG-ZHAI), on the eastern shore of Lake Beihai, north of the Spring Rain Forest Lake. Now in course of restoration, the garden is closed to the public.

QIAOYUAN HOTEL GARDEN. An agricultural production unit on the south side of Peking was converted into a hotel, and there in 1984 this artificial cliff was erected in the centre of a building complex.

CHANG'AN AVENUE, Peking's main east-west thoroughfare. Rocks and stone compositions are the usual complement of the benches and groves in the side-lanes of the broad avenues of the capital.

SUMMER PALACE (YIHEYUAN), on the north-west side of Peking. On 18 October 1860 a detachment of British troops, completing the havoc wrought by the French, attacked the imperial buildings on the edge of Lake Kunming (a lake made by Qubilai and several of his descendants). In the space of two days some two-thirds of the 3000 buildings were destroyed by fire. After looting, little more than the stones were left. Work of inestimable value was destroyed by the ignorant and brutal invaders.

Suzhou

LION GROVE GARDEN (SHIZILIN). Created in 1342, under the late Yuan, by the superior of a Buddhist monastery. Mentioned in the 18th century by Shen Fu, who criticized it for too great an accumulation of stones from Lake Tai. Its last owners were the family of the well-known architect I.M. Pei, who presented it to the city in 1949.

GARDEN OF HARMONY, GARDEN OF EASE, OR JOYOUS GARDEN (YIYUAN). The most recent garden of Suzhou (1875), on the site of a Ming garden. It contains Lake Tai stones from three early gardens.

GARDEN OF A HOTEL. Modern.

GARDEN OF THE MASTER OF THE FISHING NETS OR FISHERMAN'S GARDEN (WANGSHIYUAN). Begun in 1440 by a scholar of Yangzhou, abandoned for three centuries, reconstructed in 1770 and restored in 1940.

WESTERN GARDEN (XIYUAN). So named because it was originally the western part of the Garden to Linger In, given to a Buddhist monastery.

GARDEN OF THE GREEN WAVE PAVILION (CANGLANGTING). Created in 1044, destroyed and reconstructed many times. Its last reconstruction dates from 1927.

GARDEN OF THE STUPID OFFICIAL OR HUMBLE ADMINISTRATOR'S GARDEN (ZHUOZHENG-YUAN). Originally the garden of a Confucian scholar of the Tang dynasty. Converted under the Yuan to a monastery garden, then reconstructed by a scholar under the Ming. Largest of the old gardens of Suzhou, covering nearly ten acres; three-fifths of that area is occupied by lakes.

GARDEN TO LINGER IN (LIUYUAN). Ming period.

Yangzhou

RESOUNDING ROARS MOUNTAIN VILLA GARDEN (JIXIAO SHANGZHUANG). "Resounding roars" is an allusion to the ancient practice of Taoist hermits. Also known as Heyuan, this garden was created under the Qing dynasty.

ISOLATED GARDEN (GEYUAN). Dating to the middle years of the Qing dynasty, it contains some remarkable stone compositions of the four seasons.

WESTERN GARDEN (XIYUAN) OF THE GREAT BRIGHT TEMPLE (DAMING SI). The temple was founded under the Tang dynasty. The Western Garden was reconstructed in 1751 on the occasion of the Emperor Qianlong's visit to Yangzhou.

GARDEN OF THE SMALL WINDING VALLEY (XIAOPANGU). Now a rest home for high officials, closed to the public. The Emperor Qianlong, admiring the fine artificial cliff overhanging the ornamental lake, is said to have invited its maker to Peking to lay out the gardens of his Palace of Tranquil Longevity in the Forbidden City.

GARDEN OF THE SHI KEFA MEMORIAL TEMPLE (SHIGONGCI). Shi Kefa is a national hero. An official at Yangzhou under the late Ming, he attempted to commit suicide when the Qing took power. He was then arrested and executed. His body was never found, but a temple and tomb were built over the spot where his clothes were buried. The temple is now a museum.

Wuxi

PLUM GARDEN (MEIYUAN), west of the city. A modest garden under the Qing, it was enlarged in 1912 and reconstructed after 1949.

JAPAN

Unless otherwise stated, these gardens are in Kyōto.

GARDEN OF THE DAISEN-IN, one of the Zen monasteries of the DAITOKU-JI. This dry stone-and-gravel garden *(kare san sui)*, laid out in 1509 by Kogaku Sotan, founder of the temple, is sometimes attributed to the painter Sōami. It was restored in 1961 from the early plans.

GARDEN OF THE GINKAKU-JI: TEMPLE OF THE SILVER PAVILION, name given to the JISHO-IN, a residence and garden constructed by Yoshimasa between 1483 and 1489.

HŌJŌ GARDEN OF THE DAITOKU-JI. The DAITO-KU-JI is a group of twenty-four Zen monasteries of the Rinzai School, founded north of Kyōto in 1319. The Hōjō is the Superior's residence, the administrative centre.

KATSURA DETACHED PALACE GARDEN. Residence, garden and tea houses built in three stages from 1615 to 1660 by the Imperial Prince Toshihito (1579-1629) and his son Toshitada (1619-1662), south-west of Kyōto.

GARDEN OF THE KINKAKU-JI: TEMPLE OF THE GOLDEN PAVILION, name given to the ROKUON-JI. A garden originating in the Heian period. Deliberately burnt down by a Zen monk in 1950, the Golden Pavilion was rebuilt in 1951.

KISHIWADA CASTLE GARDEN, in the Kii Peninsula (Osaka urban prefecture). A modern garden created by Mirei Shigemori (completed November 1953) in the inner compound of the reconstructed feudal castle.

KOKEDERA GARDEN: MOSS TEMPLE, name given to the SAIHŌ-JI. The garden goes back to the Heian period. The temple was built in 1338 by Musō Kokushi. To him are attributed the stone compositions, thought to be the earliest of Zen inspiration.

KOKEI GARDEN, a famous site in China. Name of a garden once situated in front of Hideyoshi's reading room in Fushimi Castle and removed in 1630 to the precincts of the Nishi Hongan-ji Zen monastery, attributed to Shimano-suke Asagiri.

RYŌAN-JI GARDEN, one of the most famous Zen gardens of Kyōto, made up of fifteen stones. Date uncertain, maker unknown.

RYŌGEN-IN GARDEN, called RYŌGINTEI, a stone composition on a bed of moss attributed to the painter Sōami (1502).

SAMBŌ-IN GARDEN, not far from the town of Uji, south of Kyōto, and forming part of the DAIGO-JI Temple. Construction of this garden began in 1598 at the behest of Hideyoshi.

ENTRANCE GARDEN OF THE SŌ-JI-IN MONASTERY, one of the many monasteries at KŌYASAN, seat and centre of the Esoteric Shingon School of Buddhism on top of Mount Kōya, 60 miles south of Kyōto.

GARDEN OF THE TAIZO-IN, a Zen monastery built in 1404 in the precincts of the MYŌSHIN-JI. The garden is attributed to the painter Kanō Motonobu (1476-1559).

GARDEN OF TAKAMATSU TOWN HALL, on the island of Shikoku, the work of the architect Kenzō Tange.

GARDEN OF THE TENRYŪ-JI, THE TEMPLE OF THE CELESTIAL DRAGON, a Zen monastery of the Rinzai sect founded in 1339 by Musō Kokushi west of Kyōto.

GARDEN OF THE TŌFUKU-JI, a Zen temple and monastery south of Kyōto, founded in 1236, and main centre of the Rinzai sect. The gardens were created by Mirei Shigemori in 1938-1939.

ZUIHO-IN GARDEN, in the precincts of the DAITOKU-JI. A modern garden created by Mirei Shigemori in 1961, in front of a tea house.

BIBLIOGRAPHY

AN CHUNYANG, *Suzhou, A Garden City*, Foreign Languages Press, Peking 1984.

CHEN CONGZHOU, *The Gardens of Yangzhou* (in Chinese), Tongji University Press, Shanghai 1983.
– *On Chinese Gardens*, a series of five essays (in English and Chinese), Tongji University Press, Shanghai 1985.

Choice Paintings of the Palace Museum, Reader's Digest Association Asia Limited, Hong Kong 1981.

CAHILL James, *Chinese Painting*, Skira, Geneva–London–New York 1960, new edition 1977.
– *Hills Beyond a River: Chinese Painting of the Yuan Dynasty 1279-1368*, Weatherhill, New York 1976.
– *Parting at the Shore: Chinese Painting of the Early and Middle Ming Dynasty 1368-1580*, Weatherhill, New York 1979.

CAILLOIS Roger, *L'écriture des pierres*, Skira, Geneva 1970.

CAPRA Fritjof, *Le Tao de la physique*, Tchou, Paris 1979.

DAMISCH Hubert, *Théorie du nuage, pour une histoire de la peinture*, Seuil, Paris 1972.

DORÉ Père Henry, S.J., *Manuel des superstitions chinoises*, Centre de Publication de l'Université d'Enseignement et de Recherche Extrême-Orient–Asie du Sud-Est de l'Université de Paris, Paris and Hong Kong 1970.

ELISSEEFF Danielle and Vadime, *La civilisation de la Chine classique*, Arthaud, Paris 1981.

ENNIN, *Ennin's Diary. The Record of a Pilgrimage to China in Search of the Law*, translated by E.O. Reischauer, The Ronald Press Company, New York 1959.

GERNET Jacques, *Le Monde chinois*, Armand Colin, Paris 1972.

GRANET Marcel, *Fêtes et chansons anciennes de la Chine*, Albin Michel, Paris 1982.

HAY John, *Kernels of Energy, Bones of Earth, The Rock in Chinese Art*, exhibition catalogue, China House Gallery, China Institute in America, New York, October 1985-January 1986.

HOA Léon, *Reconstruire la Chine, trente ans d'urbanisme, 1949-1979*, Editions du Moniteur, Paris, 1981.

KAWABATA Yasunari, *Tristesse et Beauté*, Albin Michel, Paris 1985.

KESWICK Maggie, *The Chinese Garden. History, Art and Architecture*, Rizzoli, New York 1978 and Academy Editions, London 1978-1980.

KUWABARA Sumio, *Toshodai-ji. Trésors d'un temple japonais*, exhibition catalogue, Petit Palais, Paris 1977.

LIU TUN-CHEN, *Suzhou Ku Tien Yüan Lin* (in Chinese), Chinese Building Industry Press, Peking 1979.

MATSUDAIRA Narimitsu, "Le rituel des prémices au Japon," in *Bulletin de la Maison Franco-Japonaise*, new series, Vol. IV, No. 2, 1955, Tokyo 1957.

MORRIS Edwin T., *The Gardens of China. History, Art and Meaning*, Scribner's, New York 1983.

MURCK Alfreda and WEN FONG, "A Chinese Garden Court. The Astor Court at The Metropolitan Museum of Art," in *The Metropolitan Museum of Art Bulletin*, Winter 1980/81, New York.

Nagel Travel Guide *China*, Nagel, Geneva 1984.

NEEDHAM Joseph, *Science and Civilisation in China*, Cambridge University Press, 1954.

Pierres de rêve, catalogue of the Galerie Janette Ostier, Paris 1979.

Procédés secrets du Joyau Magique, Traité d'Alchimie taoïste du XIe siècle, French translation from the Chinese by Farzeen Baldrian-Hussein, Les Deux Océans, Paris 1984.

RAMBACH Pierre and Susanne, *Sakutei-ki ou Le Livre secret des Jardins japonais*, complete French version of an unpublished Japanese manuscript of the late 12th century, Skira, Geneva 1973.

RYJIK Kyril, *L'Idiot chinois*, Payot, Paris 1980.

SCHNEEBERGER Pierre-Francis, *Le Dragon*, Edition des Collections Baur, Geneva 1969.

SEGHERS Pierre, *Sagesse et poésie chinoises*, Robert Laffont, Paris 1981.

SEGALEN Victor, *Briques et tuiles*, Fata Morgana, Paris 1975 and 1980.

SHEN FU, *Six récits au fil inconstant des jours*, translated from the Chinese by Pierre Ryckmans, Christian Bourgeois, Paris 1982.

SHITAO, *Les Propos sur la peinture du moine Citrouille-amère*, translation and commentary by Pierre Ryckmans, Hermann, Paris 1984.

SIREN Oswald, *Gardens of China*, The Ronald Press Company, New York 1943-1949.

SKINNER Stephen, *The Living Earth Manual of Feng-Shui Chinese Geomancy*, Routledge & Kegan Paul, London 1982, 1984.

VAN LIER Henri, *L'animal signé*, Albert de Visscher, Rhode-Saint-Genese (Belgium) 1980.

WANG GAI, *The Mustard Seed Garden Manual of Painting (1679-1701)*, facsimile of the 1887-1888 edition with the text translated from the Chinese by Mai-Mai Sze, Princeton University Press, 1977.

YU ZHUOYUN, *Palaces of the Forbidden City*, The Viking Press, New York and Allen Lane, London 1984.

ZEAMI, *La tradition secrète du Nô*, translated by René Sieffert, Gallimard, Paris 1960.

217

LIST OF ILLUSTRATIONS

Unless otherwise indicated, all the garden photographs were taken by Pierre and Susanne Rambach between 1960 and 1985.

CHINA

PEKING:

Forbidden City 18, 19, 32-34, 47, 50

Forbidden City, Garden of the Palace of Tranquil Longevity
(Ningshougong) 15, 35, 87, 96, 131, 208

Forbidden City, Imperial Garden (Yuhuayuan) 21, 37-41, 98, 107, 136, 146

Forbidden City, Courtyard of the Palace of Inheriting Heaven
(Xuanqiong) 38, 126, 140, 142

Zhongshan Park (Memorial of Sun Yat-sen) 40, 121, 122, 142, 151

Beihai Park, Garden of Serenity Study (Jingxinzhai) 22, 72, 73, 88, 102, 120

Beihai Park, Garden of the Painted Boat Retreat (Huafangzhai) . . 13, 85, 120
Qiaoyuan Hotel Garden 13
Chang'an Avenue 13
Summer Palace (Yiheyuan) 18, 30, 36, 42, 46, 130, 143, 146, 148

SUZHOU:

Lion Grove Garden (Shizilin) 82, 91, 100, 123, 134-136, 138

Garden of Harmony (Yiyuan) 99, 139, 157
Garden of a hotel. Modern 12
Garden of the Master of the Fishing Nets (Wangshiyuan) 7-9, 84, 93, 97, 144, 145, 147, 148

Western Garden (Xiyuan) 34, 107, 144
Garden of the Green Wave Pavilion (Canglangting) 89, 140
Garden of the Stupid Official (Zhuozhengyuan) 24
Garden to Linger In (Liuyuan) 23, 90, 99, 132, 149, 205

Garden of the Great Pagoda of the Temple of Gratitude (Baoen si) . 152

YANGZHOU:

Resounding Roars Mountain Villa Garden (Jixiao Shanzhuang) . . 94, 113-115
Isolated Garden (Geyuan) 102-104, 108, 109, 111, 112, 127, 141

Western Garden (Xiyuan) of the Great Bright Temple (Daming si) . 106, 121
Garden of the Small Winding Valley (Xiaopangu) 76, 77, 88, 101, 125

Garden of the Shi Kefa Memorial Temple (Shigongci) 88, 89, 206, 207

WUXI:

Plum Garden (Meiyuan) 129

JAPAN

KYŌTO:

Garden of the Daisen-in, at the Daitoku-ji 193, 196-199

Garden of the Ginkaku-ji (Temple of the Silver Pavilion) 164, 165

Hōjō Garden of the Daitoku-ji 200, 201

Garden of the Kinkaku-ji (Temple of the Golden Pavilion), name
    given to the Rokuon-ji 169

Garden of the Kokedera (Moss Temple), name given to the Saihō-ji 177, 180, 181

Katsura Detached Palace Garden 155

Kokei Garden, at the Nishi Hongan-ji 187

Ryōan-ji Garden 203

Ryōgen-in Garden, at the Daitoku-ji 183, 209

Taizo-in Garden, at the Myōshin-ji 188, 190

Tenryū-ji Garden (Temple of the Celestial Dragon) 185

Tōfuku-ji Garden 11, 175

Zuiho-in Garden, at the Daitoku-ji 10, 157

Shinto Shrine of Shimogamo 154

OTHER PLACES:

Kishiwada Castle Garden, Kii Peninsula (Osaka Prefecture) (Photo
    Tom Hatashita) 11

Sambō-in Garden, near Uji, south of Kyōto 163

Entrance Garden of the Sō-ji-in, at Kōyasan, south of Kyōto . . . 178

Garden of Takamatsu Town Hall, island of Shikoku 12

Stone composition of the 8th century, discovered at Nara in 1976
    (Photo Nara Research Institute) 162

Burial mound of the Emperor Sujin, 5th century, Nara prefecture,
    photographed from the air (Photo Yukio Futagawa, Office du
    Livre, Fribourg) 156

PAINTINGS

Anonymous Chinese master (9th-10th century): Dragon Leaping out
    of the Water. Wall painting from Temple 19, Bäzäklik (Turfan).
    Height 25″. Indische Kunstabteilung, Staatliche Museen, Berlin
    (Photo Skira Archives) 65

Anonymous Chinese master (10th century): Landscape. Sections of a
    scroll painting. J. M. Crawford Collection, New York (Photo Skira
    Archives) 174, 184

Anonymous Chinese master (18th century): Monastery of the Great
    Bright Temple (Daming si) at Yangzhou. Plates from the album
    *Palaces of the Emperor along the Road from Peking to Suzhou, six or seven
    leagues from each other*. Each plate 9″ × 11¾″. Bibliothèque Natio-
    nale, Paris (Photos BN) 17, 62, 63, 179

Anonymous Song master: Breaking the Balustrade, detail of a hanging
    scroll. Ink and colours on silk. National Palace Museum, Taipei,
    Taiwan (Photo Skira Archives) 31

Anonymous Song master: Countless Peaks and Valleys. Hanging
    scroll, paper. 49¾″ × 19½″. National Palace Museum, Taipei,
    Taiwan (Photo of the Museum) 74

Anonymous Yuan master: Autumn Colours by a Fishing Village.
    Hanging scroll, colours on silk. 64⅜″ × 34¾″. National Palace
    Museum, Taipei, Taiwan (Photo of the Museum) 189

Anonymous Qing master: The Emperor Kangxi in Ceremonial Dress. Painting on silk. 108″ × 49½″. Old Imperial Palace Museum, Peking (Photo of the Museum) 43

Anonymous Japanese master: Bird's-eye View of the Mount Kōya Monasteries (Monastery of the Shingon sect of the Tentoku-in, Kōyasan). Detail of a kakemono 157

Chen Luo, late Ming Dynasty: The Washing of the Ink Stone. Hanging scroll, light colour on paper. 48¼″ × 20¼″. National Palace Museum, Taipei, Taiwan (Photo of the Museum) 78

Du Jin, attributed to (later 15th century), Ming Dynasty: Enjoying Antiquities. Hanging scroll, colour on silk. 49⅝″ × 73⅝″. National Palace Museum, Taipei, Taiwan (Photo of the Museum) . . . 25

Fang Congyi, late Yuan and early Ming: Immortal Mountains and Numinous Woods. 47⅜″ × 19⅞″. National Palace Museum, Taipei, Taiwan (Photo of the Museum) 192

Gu Kaishi (346-407): The Nymph of the River Luo. Copy of the 12th or 13th century. Section of a silk scroll. Height 9½″. Freer Gallery of Art, Washington, D.C. (Photo Skira Archives) 118

Guo Xi (c. 1020-1090), Song Dynasty: Early Spring, 1072. Silk scroll. 62⅜″ × 22⅞″. National Palace Museum, Taipei, Taiwan (Photo of the Museum) 86

Hong Ren (1610-1663), Qing Dynasty: Dragon Pine on the Yellow Mountain. Old Imperial Palace Museum, Peking (Photo of the Museum) 117

Jin Tingbiao, Qing Dynasty: Playing the Flute at the Enchanted Grotto. Ink on paper. Diameter 28″. National Palace Museum, Taipei, Taiwan (Photo of the Museum) 95

Kun Can (1612 - c. 1692), Qing Dynasty: High Mountains and Long Streams, view of Tiandu Peak in the Huangshan Mountains (Anhui). Hanging scroll, ink and colour on paper. 126″ × 50¼″. National Palace Museum, Taipei, Taiwan (Photo of the Museum) . 54-55

Leng Qian, attributed to (c. 1310-1371), Ming Dynasty: Mount Boyue or Jinhuashan (Anhui). Silk scroll. 33¼″ × 16⅜″. National Palace Museum, Taipei, Taiwan (Photo of the Museum) 191

Liang Kai, attributed to, Song Dynasty: Ink Portrait of an Immortal, c. 1250. Paper album leaf. 19⅛″ × 10⅞″. National Palace Museum, Taipei, Taiwan (Photo of the Museum) 182

Li Tang (1050-1130), Song Dynasty: Whispering Pines in the Mountains, 1124. Hanging scroll, ink and light colour on silk. 74″ × 55″. National Palace Museum, Taipei, Taiwan (Photo of the Museum) 133

Lu Guang, Yuan Dynasty: Pavilions and Monasteries in the Mountains of the Immortals, 1330s. Hanging scroll, colour on silk. 54⅛″ × 37⅝″. National Palace Museum, Taipei, Taiwan (Photo of the Museum) 75

Ma Wan, attributed to, Yuan Dynasty: Secluded Dwelling amid Lofty Peaks, 1349. Hanging scroll, ink on silk. 47¼″ × 22¾″. National Palace Museum, Taipei, Taiwan (Photo of the Museum) 110

Mutō Shūi (14th century): Portrait of Musō Kokushi. Hanging scroll, colour on silk. 47″ × 25⅛″. Myōshin-ji Monastery, Kyōto (Photo Skira Archives) 171

Qian Xuan, attributed to, Song Dynasty: Lu Tong Brewing Tea. Hanging scroll, ink and colour on paper. 50⅝″ × 14¾″. National Palace Museum, Taipei, Taiwan (Photo of the Museum) 195

Qiu Ying (c. 1510-1551), Ming Dynasty: Landscape in the style of Li Tang. Section of a handscroll, ink and colour on paper. Height 10″. Freer Gallery of Art, Washington, D.C. (Photo Skira Archives) 60

Ren Renfa, attributed to (1254-1327), Yuan Dynasty: A Lofty Scholar
Playing the Lute. Hanging scroll, colour on silk. 57⅝″ × 22″. National Palace Museum, Taipei, Taiwan (Photo of the Museum)   .   124

Sesshū Tōyō (1420-1506): Landscape in the Cursive Style (Hoboku-sansui), 1495. Hanging scroll, ink on paper. 58¾″ × 12⅞″. National Museum, Tokyo (Photo Skira Archives)   173

Shen Zhou (1427-1509), Ming Dynasty: Lofty Mount Lu, 1467. Hanging scroll, ink and light colour on paper. 76¼″ × 38⅝″. National Palace Museum, Taipei, Taiwan (Photo of the Museum)   57

Sōtatsu (active c. 1630): Pine Islands (Matsushima). Right side of a screen painting, colours on paper. 65⅜″ × 144¾″. Freer Gallery of Art, Washington (Photo Skira Archives)   153

Sōyū (mid-16th century): Poet Contemplating a Waterfall. Japanese painting in the Chinese style. Seikadō Foundation, Tokyo   .   .   .   168

Sumiyoshi Gukei (1631-1705): Illustration of the *Tale of Genji (Genji monogatari)*. Ink and colour on paper. 14″ × 53½″. Galerie Janette Ostier, Paris (Photo Nelly Delay)   160-161

Tanaka, Junyo (20th century): The ideogram *Mu* (emptiness). Calligraphy. 53″ × 27¼″. Pierre and Susanne Rambach Collection, Geneva (Photo Christian Poite, Geneva)   176

Tang Dai and Shen Yuan: Four views from two watercolour albums, *Yuan Ming Yuan, Summer Palace near Peking and Outskirts. 40 topographical views*, 1744. Bibliothèque Nationale, Paris (Photos BN)   67, 68, 70, 71

Tang Yin (1470-1524), Ming Dynasty: Tao Gu Composing a Lyric. Hanging scroll, color on silk. 66½″ × 40¼″. National Palace Museum, Taipei, Taiwan (Photo of the Museum)   81

Wang Fu (1362-1416), Ming Dynasty: Literary Meeting in a Mountain Lodge. Hanging scroll, light color on paper. 51″ × 20¼″. National Palace Museum, Taipei, Taiwan (Photo of the Museum)   190

Wang Hui (1632-1717), Qing Dynasty: Water and Marsh Landscape in the style of Zhao Danian. Old Imperial Palace Museum, Peking (Photo of the Museum)   58

Wang Meng (1309-1385): Forest Dwellings at Zhu Chu. Hanging scroll, ink and color on paper. 27″ × 16¾″. National Palace Museum, Taipei, Taiwan (Photo Skira Archives)   137

Wang Shen, Northern Song Dynasty: Misty Landscape of Tiered Mountains and Rivers. Silk scroll. 17¾″ × 65¼″. Shanghai Museum (Photo of the Museum)   119

Wang Yun (1652-1735), Qing Dynasty: Landscape. Hanging scroll, ink and colour on silk. 23⅛″ × 11½″. National Palace Museum, Taipei, Taiwan (Photo of the Museum)   105

You Qiu (16th century), Ming Dynasty: Elegant Gathering in the Western Garden. Hanging scroll, ink on paper. 42″ × 12½″. National Palace Museum, Taipei, Taiwan (Photo of the Museum)   .   83

Yuan Jiang, Qing Dynasty: Landscape in the Eastern Garden. Detail of a silk scroll. Shanghai Museum (Photo of the Museum)   .   .   .   84

Yu Jian, Southern Song Dynasty. Mountains with Snowy Peaks. Painting of the Chan School (Photo Giraudon, Paris)   172

Zhang Ruoai (1713-1746), Qing Dynasty: Figure in the Snow. Hanging scroll, ink on paper. 44¼″ × 11¼″. National Palace Museum, Taipei, Taiwan (Photo of the Museum)   92

Zhan Ziqian (551-604 or late 7th century): Spring Travellers. Copy after his painting in the Old Imperial Palace Museum, Peking. Detail of a silk scroll. Shanghai Museum (Photo of the Museum)   .   .   61

Zhou Chen (1450-1535), Ming Dynasty: Leisurely Watching Children Collect Willow Flowers. Hanging scroll, colour on silk. 46″ × 25″. National Palace Museum, Taipei, Taiwan (Photo of the Museum)   122

– Arrival of a Visitor at a Mountain Hermitage. Silk scroll.
53¾" × 28½". Shanghai Museum (Photo of the Museum) . . .   128

Zhou Wenju, attributed to, Southern Tang (Five Dynasties): Watching the Ducks at the Water Pavilion, c. 970. Colour on silk. 9⅝" × 10½". National Palace Museum, Taipei, Taiwan (Photo of the Museum)   116

CHINESE BOOKS

Plates from Wang Gai's *Mustard Seed Garden Manual of Painting*, 1679   20, 48, 79, 121, 170

Woodcut from the *Xixiangji* published during the Wanli era, Ming Dynasty, between 1573 and 1619   22

Woodcut from the *Xixiangji* published during the Chongzhen era, Ming Dynasty, between 1628 and 1643 . . . .   136, 137

Schematic model of the general relief of the Chinese land mass and Map showing population density, from Leon Hoa, *Reconstruire la Chine*, Paris 1981 . . . .   48, 49

How to draw the imperial dragon motif. Illustration from an article by Yin Yuanzhen of the costume workshop of the Peking Opera . .   49

Plate from the *Chuci* published under the Qing, 1645   53

Siting of the Dragon's Lair according to a Fengshui manual   . . .   61

Didactic drawing from a 19th century book on garden design in ancient China, from *On Chinese Gardens* by Chen Congzhou, Shanghai 1985   64

Woodcut from the *Yuchuyi*, a book of extraordinary stories, published under the Ming, 1606 . . . .   104, 130, 144, 145

Plate from the *Hongfuji*, a book of extraordinary tales in two volumes, published under the Ming, 1601   149

Plate from the *15th Notebook of Chinese Gardens. Gardens of the Emperor of China in 28 plates*, engraved by Le Rouge, 1786 (Photo Christian Poite, Geneva)   69

JAPANESE BOOKS

Plates from the *Kyōto Garden Book*, 1830 . . . .   166, 167, 194

Plate from Vol. III of the *Tsukiyama Niwatsukushi no den* (Building Tradition of Artificial Mountains and Gardens) by Sigeyoshi, 1735   197

Plate from a book by Suzuki Harunobu (Photo Skira Archives) . .   202

OBJECTS

Chinese make-up box, reign of Qianlong (1736-1795). Cloisonné enamel. Diameter 4¼". Baur Collections, Geneva (Photo Pierre-Alain Ferrazzini)   44

Chinese geomancer's compass (*luopan*) of varnished wood with eight reading rings. Contemporary work. Life-size. Gilbert Mazliah Collection (Photo Christian Poite, Geneva)   59

Chinese ink palette found in a tomb at Zhongbao (Shaanxi), 8th century. Three-colour ware   64

Chinese dreamstone signed Wang Yu. Dark-veined marble heightened with painting. Diameter 9¼". Galerie Janette Ostier, Paris (Photo Laurent Chastel)   26

Two Chinese dreamstones in the Residence of the Garden of the Master of the Fishing Nets, Suzhou. Height c. 31½″ 28, 29

Chinese dreamstone inscribed in the usual style, unsigned. Grey-veined marble. Diameter 4¾″. Pierre and Susanne Rambach Collection, Geneva (Photo Christian Poite) 52

Chinese dreamstone in the Residence of the Garden of the Master of the Fishing Nets, Suzhou 27

Chinese porcelain vase with red-copper underpainting, reign of Kangxi (1662-1722). Height 8⅞″. Baur Collections, Geneva (Photo Pierre-Alain Ferrazzini) 51

SCULPTURES

Cloud dragon stele, Twin Pagodas (Shangta si), Suzhou 51

Woodcarving in the former residence of the king of the Taiping, now the Municipal Museum, Suzhou 80

Shiva dancing, 10th century. From the Temple of Mukteswar, Bhubaneswar (Orissa province, India) 150

Portrait of the Monk Jianzhen (Ganjin). Dry-lacquered wood, overpainted in colours 159

INDEX

Chinese words are here transcribed in accordance with the *pinyin* system,
the alphabetical script adopted by the People's Republic of China.

Ama-no-hashidate (Bridge of Heaven), one of the three most famous sites in Japan. It is a sandbank in the Sea of Japan, 2 miles long, 140 miles wide, covered with storm-twisted pines. A site often evoked by painters and garden masters 155.

Amida, personification of the Buddhist ideal; not a historical figure. His worshippers will be reborn in his Pure Land paradise–image of the plane of consciousness to which those accede who have achieved Awakening 14, 204.

Arashiyama, hill west of Kyōto, bringing together all the beauties of nature 186, 200.

Astor Court, Metropolitan Museum of Art, New York 8.

Attiret, Jean-Denis (1702-1768), Jesuit and painter at the court of the Emperor Qianlong. He took part in decorating the Italian-style buildings erected near the Summer Palaces 69.

Bai Juyi (772-846), famous poet of the Tang period 42.

Bäzäklik (Central Asia), on the Silk Road near the Turfan oasis. Monastic centre with frescoes in an Indo-Iranian style marked by Chinese influence 64, 65, 69, 77.

Beihai (North Sea), one of the artificial lakes west of the Forbidden City 66, 72.

Bianliang, Northern Song capital south of the Yellow River. Now called Kaifeng, capital of Henan 17, 39.

Bodhidharma (6th century), Indian monk traditionally said to have introduced into China the methods and aims of meditation (in Sanscrit *dhyāna*, in Chinese *chan*, in Japanese *zen*) 172.

Bon seki, Japanese art of harmoniously arranging pebbles on a tray 202.

Book of Changes or *Yi Jing (I Ching)* 49, 51.

Cahill, James (born California, 1926), Professor of Art History at the University of California, Berkeley, and a leading authority on Chinese painting 108, 119, 182.

Canglangting, Garden of the Green Wave Pavilion, Suzhou (see List of Gardens) 89, 140.

Chan (in Sanscrit *dhyāna*, from the root *dyā*, to think), meditation. Ecstatic state of mind in which one awakes to Knowledge. School of Buddhism founded in China by the Indian monk Bodhidharma in the 6th century. Brought to Japan in the 12th century by the Japanese monk Eisai and known there as Zen 172, 173, 175, 178, 182, 184, 192, 204.

Chang'an, on the site of present-day Xian (Shaanxi), one of the foremost cultural centres of ancient China and capital from 1122 B.C. to the end of the Tang dynasty (A.D. 907) 158.

Chang'an Avenue, Peking (see List of Gardens) 13.

Chen Congzhou, Professor of the History of Architecture, Tongji University, Shanghai, author of many studies of Chinese gardens (see Bibliography) 12, 90, 116.

Chen Luo, Ming painter 78.

Chen Zi'ang (661-702), Tang poet 120.

Confucius (in Chinese Kong qiu, c. 551-c. 479 B.C.), the father of Chinese philosophy 16, 80, 82, 148.

Daisen-in, Zen monastery, Kyōto (see List of Gardens) 191, 193, 196-200.

Daitoku-ji, group of Zen monasteries, Kyōto (see List of Gardens) 10, 11, 183, 186, 193, 194, 200, 201, 209.

Daming si, Great Bright Temple, Yangzhou (see List of Gardens) 16, 17, 106, 107, 120, 121, 210.

Damisch, Hubert (born 1928), teaches the theory and history of art at the Ecole Pratique des Hautes Etudes and the Ecole Normale Supérieure, Paris (see Bibliography) 130.

Dōgen, Japanese monk, in China from 1123 to 1127, founder of the Soto Zen School 173, 178.

Du Jin, called Yaonan. Lived at Chang'an during the Chinghua era (1465-1487), then having failed the civil examinations, he devoted himself to painting, chiefly figure painting 25.

Eisai or Ensai (1141-1215), Japanese monk of the Tendai sect. Studied the doctrines of the master Linzi at a Chan monastery in China. Returning to Japan in 1191, he founded the School of Rinzai Zen Buddhism 173, 178.

Ennin (794-864), Japanese monk of the Tendai sect. After nine years in China, he brought back to Japan the practice of meditating on the name of Amida. Wrote an account of his pilgrimage to China (see Bibliography) 16, 178.

Fang Congyi, Yuan painter still alive in early Ming times. A Taoist priest from his youth, he spent most of his life in a temple in Jiangxi 192.

Fanghu, one of the three mystical Isles of the Immortals, located in the Gulf of Bohai 140.

Ganjin, see Jianzhen.

Ge Gong (4th century A.D.), Chinese alchemist 94.

Gemmyō (661-721), Empress of Japan. In 710 she founded the first fixed capital, Heijo-kyō 158.

Genji monogatari (Tale of Genji), a famous novel of the early 11th century by Murasaki Shikibu, lady-in-waiting at the Heian court 160, 161.

Gernet, Jacques, Professor at the University of Paris VII, director of studies at the Ecole Pratique des Hautes Etudes 48.

Geyuan, Isolated Garden, Yangzhou (see List of Gardens) 16, 102-104, 108-112, 127, 141.

Ginkaku-ji, Temple of the Silver Pavilion, Kyōto (see List of Gardens) 164, 165.

Gokyōhoko, Yoshitsune (died 1206), said to have written the *Sakutei-ki* 14.

Granet, Marcel (1884-1940), French sinologist (see Bibliography) 80.

Guilin (Guangxi province). The strange landscape around this city made it a favourite with painters and poets 27.

Gu Kaizhi (346-407), Six Dynasties painter, the most famous of Chinese figure painters. His work is only known today from copies, some of them very old 118.

Guo Xi (c. 1020-1090), Song painter who powerfully dominated his time, and author of the *Linquan Gaozhi*, the most important Chinese treatise on landscape 74, 86.

Han empire (2nd century B.C.-2nd century A.D.) 59, 80, 142.

Hangzhou (Lin'an), city founded in 606 at the end-point of the Grand Canal, capital of the Southern Song dynasty (1127-1279) 17, 142.

Harunobu, see Suzuki Harunobu.

Hatashita, Tom, Japanese-Canadian architect and garden designer. Lives in Toronto, has worked in Kyōto, New Delhi, Paris and Kinshasa 12.

Heian-kyō (Peace Capital), old name of Kyōto, founded in 794 158.

Heilongjiang, one of the three north-eastern provinces of China, part of what Westerners call Manchuria 48.

Heyuan, or Jixiao Shanzhuang, Yangzhou (see List of Gardens) 16.

Hideyoshi, Toyotomi (1536-1598), general in chief (Shōgun) and dictator of Japan from 1584 to his death 163, 202.

Hindu Kush, mountain system lying mainly in north-eastern Afghanistan, the western extension of the Himalayas 45.

Hoa, Leon, one of the chief architects of the Architectural Planning Institute, Peking (see Bibliography) 60.

Hong Ren (1610-1663), Qing painter, one of the most introspective and fascinating of the 17th century. After the fall of the Ming, he withdrew to a monastery and till his death painted landscape elements: trees, mountains, rocks. Instead of representing them, he presented them as vessels of the Breath Force and microcosms of the Universe 117.

Horai, Japanese name of the Isle or Mountain of the Immortals in Chinese mythology 10, 180.

Horyū-ji, temple founded at Nara in 607. Considered the oldest group of wooden buildings in the world, the work of Korean architects and carpenters 158.

Huafangzhai, Painted Boat Retreat, Peking (see List of Gardens) 13, 85, 120.

Huanghe, Yellow River, second longest in China (c. 2900 miles) 16, 17, 53.

Huizong, last Northern Song emperor (1101-1125), himself an outstanding painter, calligrapher and connoisseur of the arts 38, 39.

Ise peninsula (southern Honshū), important Shintō centre, with shrines to the sun goddess Amaterasu, ancestor of the imperial family. Founded in the 6th century, the Ise temples are destroyed and rebuilt every twenty years 158.

Izanagi and Izaname, brother and sister, divine Shintō couple. All Japan (islands, beings, things) was the fruit of their union 154.

Jiangzi, Blue River, China 16.

Jianzhen (Ganjin in Japanese, 688-763), Chinese monk of the Liu sect (Ritsu in Japanese) which he brought to Japan. After several abortive attempts, he finally reached Japan in 753. At Nara in 759 he founded the Tōshōdai-ji 16, 17, 158, 159, 210.

Jin Tingbiao (18th century), court painter of the Emperor Qianlong. Recruited by the latter during a journey to South China and much appreciated by him: witness the poems written by the emperor on some of the painter's works after his death 95.

Jing Hao (early 10th century), one of the most important painters of a period which marked a decisive turning point in the evolution of Chinese painting. Author of the *Bifa Ji*, a treatise on painting 206.

Jingxinzhai, Garden of Serenity Study, Peking (see List of Gardens) 22, 72, 73, 77, 88, 99, 102, 120, 124.

Jixiao Shanzhuang, Resounding Roars Mountain Villa Garden, Yangzhou (see List of Gardens) 94, 113-115.

Jürchen, tribes of Tungus horsemen on the northern confines of China, who in 1126 captured Kaifeng, the Song capital. Ancestors of the tribes who in the early 17th century adopted the name Manchu 38.

Kaifeng, see Bianliang.

Kami, Shintō divinities. Spirits of ancestors, clan chiefs, village headmen. Spirits dwelling in trees, springs, rivers, mountains, stones 154, 156, 161, 163, 166, 180, 184, 206.

Kangxi, Manchu Qing emperor (1662-1722) 43, 51.

Kanō Motonobu (1476-1559), son of Masanobu and founder of the Kanō school of painting 188.

Kare san sui, Japanese dry-stone garden (*kare*, dry; *san sui*, mountain, water). In such gardens, water is represented by gravel or moss 92.

Katsura Garden, Kyōto (see List of Gardens) 155.

Kawabata, Yasunari, Nobel prize for literature in 1968, committed suicide on 16 April 1972 180.

Kinkaku-ji, Kyōto (see List of Gardens) 166, 167, 169.

Kishiwada Garden, Osaka prefecture (see List of Gardens) 10, 11.

Kōbo Daishi (774-835), posthumous title of Kukai, a Buddhist monk who went to China in 804 and thence brought the Shingon sect to Japan. Founder of the Kōyasan monasteries 157, 173.

Kojiki, first historical chronicles of Japan, relating the formation of the Nippon State from the legendary creation of the islands to the reign of the Empress Suiko (A.D. 592-628) 154, 199.

Kokedera, Moss Temple, Kyōto (see List of Gardens) 176, 177.

Kokei, Kyōto (see List of Gardens) 187.

Kōtoku, 36th Emperor of Japan (A.D. 645-654) 158.

Kōyasan (Mount Kōya), sacred mountain at Wakayama where in 816 the monk Kukai founded the centre of the Shingon School of Esoteric Buddhism 156, 157, 178.

Kukai, see Kōbo Daishi.

Kun Can (1612-c. 1692), one of the four famous painter monks of the Qing dynasty, with Hong Ren, Bada Shanren and Shitao 54, 55.

Kunlun, mountain range separating Tibet from Chinese Turkistan. In the Taoist cosmogony, Kunlun designates the axis of the world 35, 118.

226

Kyūshū, southernmost of the four main islands of the Japanese archipelago 158.

Laozi (6th or 5th century B.C.), Chinese philosopher, founder of Taoism and presumed author of the *Daodejing* (Book of the Way and of Virtue) 16, 20, 36, 82, 113, 200.

Legalists, School of. Doctrine of government based on the principle that, since man is not naturally good, order can only be maintained by a strict system of laws, rewards, and punishments 80.

Leng Qian (c. 1310-1371), late Yuan and early Ming painter. Under the Yuan he was a Taoist monk living aloof in the Wu mountains near Hangzhou. When this Mongol dynasty was driven out, he was summoned to court as an expert on music. Tradition credits him with magical powers 191.

Liang Kai (mid-13th century). A much esteemed official painter, he left the Song court and withdrew to a Chan monastery where he created a free style, seeking not to please but to express the underlying nature of being, the *Qi* (Breath Force) 178, 182.

Linzi (died 866), one of the most famous Chan masters of the Tang period. From his teaching, brought back to Japan (where he was called Rinzai) by Eisai in 1191, arose the Rinzai School of Zen Buddhism. He is known to us from the *Conversations* recorded by one of his disciples 173.

Li Tang (1050-1130), Song painter from Henan and member of the Imperial Academy of Bianliang (Kaifeng). Following the court to Hangzhou, he there imposed a style of painting which prevailed till the fall of the dynasty 60, 133.

Liuyuan, Garden to Linger In, Suzhou (see List of Gardens) 23, 90, 99, 132, 149, 205.

Lu, kingdom in Shandong, native state of Confucius 80.

Lu Guang (14th century), Yuan painter 75.

Matsudaira, Narimitsu, doctor of the University of Paris and professor at the Metropolitan University of Tokyo (see Bibliography) 155.

Ma Wan (active 1342-1365), late Yuan painter, poet, calligrapher and author 110.

Meiji era (1868-1912) in Japan 8.

Meishan (Coal Hill), north of the Forbidden City 59, 66.

Meiyuan, Plum Garden, Wuxi (see List of Gardens) 129.

Mengzi or Mencius (372-289 B.C.), Chinese philosopher, second only to Confucius 80.

Mi Fu (1051-1107), famous scholar, calligrapher, painter, antiquarian and collector, one of those flamboyant personalities who did so much to shape the tastes of the Chinese patrician. Author of critical essays on the paintings familiar to him in his day 78, 79.

Ming dynasty (1368-1644), following that of the Mongols (Yuan) and preceding that of the Manchus (Qing) 8, 16, 18, 21, 22, 25, 57, 60, 78, 80, 83, 104, 122, 128, 130, 136, 144, 149, 175, 188, 190, 192, 206.

Momoyama period (1573-1603) in Japan, following the Kamakura period and preceding the Edo period 202.

Mori, Osamu, contemporary historian and garden specialist in Japan 162.

Musō Kokushi (1275-1351), also called Soseki, first abbot of the Tenryū-ji Zen monastery, Kyōto, creator of its stone gardens and those of the Saihō-ji 171, 176, 177, 180, 181, 184, 185.

Mutō Shūi (14th century), Japanese painter 171.

Myōshin-ji, group of Rinzai Zen monasteries at Kyōto 186, 188, 190

Naniwa, first fixed but shortlived capital of Japan, founded in 646 by the Emperor Kōtoku on the present site of Osaka 158.

Nara period (710-794) in Japan, preceding the Heian period. From the end of the Nara period, Kyōto was the capital of Japan 158.

Nara (central Honshū), city erected on the site of Heijo-kyō and capital of Japan from 710 to 794 158, 162, 164, 178, 202, 210.

Needham, Joseph (born London, 1900), former head of the British Scientific Mission to China (see Bibliography) 148.

New York, Chase Manhattan Bank 12.

New York, Metropolitan Museum of Art, Astor Court 8.

Ningshougong, Palace of Tranquil Longevity, Peking (see List of Gardens) 14, 15, 35, 84, 87, 96, 131, 208.

Niwa, Japanese word once meaning the space cleared at the foot of a mountain as a place of welcome for the *kami*. Today it means garden 156.

Noguchi, Isamu (born Los Angeles, 1904), Japanese-American sculptor and landscape gardener 12.

Paris, Unesco Building 12.

Penglai, one of the three mythical Isles of the Immortals located in the Gulf of Bohai 140.

Polo, Marco (1254-1324), Venetian traveller to China where he served the Mongol emperor Qubilai (Kublai Khan). Returned to Venice in 1295, and while in prison in Genoa in 1298 he dictated an account of his experiences 16, 17.

Qianlong, Qing dynasty emperor (1736-1796), an enlightened despot, great builder and art lover 19, 44, 66, 69, 72, 84, 96, 178, 184.

Qian Xuan (c. 1235-1301), late Song and early Yuan painter 195.

Qiaoyuan Hotel, Peking (see List of Gardens) 13.

Qin, cithara about four feet long with seven silk strings, the favourite musical instrument of the Chinese scholar, present at all poetic or religious gatherings calling for composure, silence and peace of mind 24, 25.

Qing, Manchu dynasty (1644-1850) following that of the Ming and preceding Western ascendancy 43, 53, 55, 58, 83, 92, 94, 105, 116, 206.

Qiu Ying (c. 1510-1551), Ming painter, uncle of You Qiu 60, 68.

Qubilai (Kublai Khan, 1214-1294), grandson of Jenghiz Khan. Emperor (1260-1294) and founder of the Mongol (Yuan) dynasty of China 16, 66.

227

Ren Renfa (1254-1327), Yuan literati painter in the service of the Mongols, best known for his pictures of horses 124.

Rokuon-ji, see Kinkaku-ji.

Ryckmans, Pierre, Belgian sinologist, professor at the University of Canberra (see Bibliography) 54, 74, 113, 130, 206.

Ryjik, Kyril, professor of Chinese philosophy at the Polytechnic Institute of Philosophy, University of Paris VIII (see Bibliography) 35.

Ryōan-ji, Kyōto (see List of Gardens) 202, 203.

Ryōgen-in, Kyōto (see List of Gardens) 183, 209.

Saichō (767-822), Japanese Buddhist monk, founder of the Tendai sect after a sojourn in the Chinese monasteries of Mount Tian Tai 173.

Saihō-ji or Kokedera, Moss Temple, Kyōto (see List of Gardens) 176, 177, 180, 181.

Sakutei-ki (Notes on the Making of Gardens), also known as *Zen sai hisho* (Summary of the Secrets of Garden Construction), a Japanese manuscript of the late 12th century, possibly written by Yoshitsuna Tachibana (see Bibliography) 12, 14, 20, 156, 160, 162, 163, 166, 180, 200, 201, 204.

Sambō-in, near Kyōto (see List of Gardens) 163.

San zon seki (three saint stones), grouping of three stones in Japanese gardens, symbolizing Buddha and three attendants 196, 200.

Satori, Japanese term meaning Buddhist Awakening 173, 176.

Schneeberger, Pierre-Francis, former curator of the Baur Collections, Geneva (see Bibliography) 45, 46.

Segalen, Victor (1878-1919), French writer and ship's doctor, in China from 1908 to 1914 (see Bibliography) 136.

Seimu, Emperor of Japan who founded the capitals of Kuni (740), Shigaraki (742), Naniwa (744) and rebuilt Heijo (Nara) in 745 158.

Sesshū Tōyō (1420-1506), considered by the Japanese as their greatest painter. A Zen monk and Chinese scholar, he spent several years in China (1467-1469) and made the journey from Hangzhou to Peking 173.

Shen Fu, a scholar of the later 18th century, a native of Suzhou and author of a famous autobiography (see Bibliography) 82, 113, 142.

Shen Zhou (1427-1509), Ming painter born into one of the most distinguished families of Suzhou. He devoted his life to poetry, painting, calligraphy and his mother (who became a centenarian). Not till forty did Shen Zhou tackle works of any size 57.

Shigemori, Mirei (born 1896), one of the outstanding Japanese garden designers of this century. Author of many books on gardens, including a seven-volume survey of all the older gardens (not translated). A creator of new forms, who has helped to renovate many of the Kyōto gardens 10-12, 157, 162, 175, 180.

Shigongci, Shi Kefa Temple, Yangzhou (see List of Gardens) 88, 89, 109, 206, 207.

Shi Huang di (3rd century B.C.), first Emperor and unifier of China 20.

Shi Kefa, Yangzhou (see List of Gardens) 88, 89, 206.

Shiko, Japanese name of Shi Huang di, first Emperor of China, who burnt the books in 213 B.C. 20.

Shimogamo, Shintō shrine north of Kyōto 154, 199.

Shingon, esoteric sect of Japanese Buddhism, founded by Kukai after his return from China in 806 157, 173, 176, 204.

Shitao (1630?-1720?), painter and theorist of painting, author of *Remarks on Painting by the Monk Bitter Pumpkin*, published in 1728 (see Bibliography) 16, 54, 58, 74, 96, 120, 130, 136, 188, 190, 191.

Shiva, one of the Hindu trinity (Brahma the creator, Vishnu the preserver, Shiva the destroyer). But in the reviving Brahmanism of the Middle Ages, Shiva is more prominent, becoming for many the supreme god. He then became the god of both destruction and creation. This dual, simultaneous aspect is symbolically represented by the dance of Shiva. The contrast between his moving limbs and motionless face expresses the paradox of time and eternity, of mortal existence and indestructible selfhood 36, 150.

Shizilin, Lion Grove Garden, Suzhou (see List of Gardens) 82, 91, 100, 123, 134-136, 138, 145.

Shōtoku (574-622), nephew and regent of the Empress Suiko, founder of a Japanese state on Chinese lines, and great protector of Buddhism 158.

Sima Qian (born 145 B.C.), historian of the Han dynasty and author of a general history of China down to his time *(Historical Memoirs)* 140.

Simonet, Jean-Marie, scientific director of the Institut Belge des Hautes Etudes Chinoises 21.

Sōami (1472-1523), Japanese painter and garden designer 193, 202.

Sō-ji-in, Kōyasan monastery (see List of Gardens) 178.

Song or Sung dynasty, founded in 960 and partially collapsing in 1125 under the Jürchen invasions. The Southern Song government, reconstituted at Hangzhou, lasted till 1276 17, 31, 39, 74, 83, 86, 119, 132, 149, 172, 178, 182, 184, 195.

Sōseki, see Musō Kokushi.

Sōtatsu (active c. 1630), Japanese painter 153.

Sōyū (mid-16th century), Japanese painter 166, 168.

Su Dongpo, see Su Shi.

Su Shi (Su Dongpo, 1036-1101), the most representative Chinese writer of the Song period, in both prose and poetry. Opposed, like most of the literati of his time, to the reform movement of Wang Anshi, he spent the greater part of his administrative career in provincial posts, a career replete with disappointments and rebuffs. But he was sensible and strong-minded enough always to look up, not down, and found consolation in nature, friendship, poetry and philosophy 38, 83.

Sui dynasty (A.D. 581-618), founded by General Yang Kien, who reunified the empire, putting an end to the troubled Six Dynasties period 16, 180.

Sujin, Emperor of Japan (5th century) 156.

Sumiyoshi Gukei (1631-1705), Japanese painter 160, 161.

Suzuki Harunobu (1725-1770), Japanese print designer specializing in feminine figures 202.

Taiping Rebellion (1850-1864), a political and religious uprising against the Qing regime 16, 80.

Taizo-in, Kyōto (see List of Gardens) 188, 190.

Takamatsu, island of Shikoku (see List of Gardens) 11, 12.

Tanaka, Junyo, Japanese monk of Kōyasan. Now living in New York where he teaches the Shingon ritual   176.

Tang dynasty (618-917), capital Chang'an, then Luoyang. Followed the Sui and preceded the Five Dynasties   16, 24, 38, 64, 69, 116, 119, 146, 158, 210.

Tange, Kenzō (born 1914), Japanese architect, a figure of international importance in modern architecture since the 1950s   11, 12.

Tangshan, city in Hebei province, north-east of Tianjin, largely destroyed by an earthquake in 1976   20.

Tang Yin (1470-1524), considered by Chinese critics as one of the four greatest Ming painters. Son of a Suzhou merchant, he took first place twice in provincial examinations, the first time when he was only fifteen. But his career as a government official was early ruined when he was involved in a financial scandal. He then devoted himself to painting   80, 81.

Tao or Dao, the Way. Hence the term Taoism, coined in the 19th century. See Zhuangzi   27, 45, 52, 59, 64, 82, 172, 173, 200, 209.

Tao Gu (1470-1524), Ming painter born at Suzhou   80, 81.

Taoism, one of the two standbys of the Chinese mind (the other being Confucianism), based on the teachings of Laozi in the *Daodejing* (Book of the Way and of Virtue) and of Zhuangzi in the book that bears his name   80, 82, 92, 96, 102, 119, 146, 148, 172, 173, 184, 191, 204.

Tao Yuanming (A.D. 365-427), poet of the countryside and chrysanthemums. A major influence on Chinese poetry, and many painters, such as Shitao, were inspired by his poems   124.

Tendai School of Buddhism, founded in Japan in the early 9th century by the monk Saichō (better known by his posthumous name, Dengyō Daishi). A syncretic school, reducing the varied mass of Buddhist theories to a single system   173, 204.

Tenno-ji, Japanese temple founded in 593 by Prince Shōtoku (573-621). It has now completely disappeared   156.

Tenryū-ji, Kyōto (see List of Gardens)   175, 176, 184-186, 200.

Tōfuku-ji, Kyōto (see List of Gardens)   10, 11, 175.

Torii, wooden, stone or bronze portico, marking the entrance to the pure zones surrounding Shintō shrines   166.

Tōshōdai-ji, Nara, main temple of the Ritsu sect. Founded in 759 by the Chinese monk Jianzhen (Ganjin)   158, 210.

Vandier-Nicolas, Nicole, contemporary French sinologist, author of many books on the literati aesthetic   130.

Viçakhadatta (6th century), Hindu poet   150.

Wang Fu (1362-1416), Ming poet, painter and calligrapher, born at Wuxi. Kept to the literati tradition of the Yuan when the trend was all for a return to the Southern Song style   188, 190.

Wang Gai (18th century), Chinese painter and theorist (see Bibliography)   20, 48, 79, 121, 170.

Wang Hui (1632-1717), Qing painter famous for his ability to reproduce any painting in any style, without adding anything of his own   58.

Wang Meng (1309-1385), born into a family of painters, south of Lake Tai, and considered one of the greatest of the later Yuan painters. The first to treat a mountain as a huge living organism. He died in prison   137.

Wang Shen, Northern Song painter   83, 119.

Wangshiyuan, Garden of the Master of the Fishing Nets, Suzhou (see List of Gardens)   7-9, 27-29, 84, 92, 93, 97, 144-148.

Wang Xizhi (A.D. 307-365), honoured as the greatest master of Chinese calligraphy. Recorded in 353 as bringing together forty of his literati friends to celebrate the end of spring, sitting together under the trees by a winding stream   96.

Wang Yun (1652-1735), early Qing painter, born into a family of painters. His buildings and figures are said to be in the style of Qiu Ying, his landscapes in that of Shen Zhou   104, 105.

Wu, old name of the region south of the lower course of the Blue River (Jiangzi)   17.

Xia dynasty (c. 2200-1800 B.C.), traditionally the first of Chinese history, going back to Late Neolithic times, founded by the mythical hero Yu the Great   66.

Xiaopangu, Garden of the Small Winding Valley, Yangzhou (see List of Gardens)   16, 74, 76, 77, 88, 101, 125, 186.

Xie He (active c. A.D. 500), painter and theorist, author of the earliest extant treatise on painting   209.

Xiyuan, Western Garden, Suzhou (see List of Gardens)   34, 107, 144.

Xiyuan, Western Garden, Yangzhou (see List of Gardens)   106, 120.

Xuanqiong, Courtyard of the Palace of Inheriting Heaven, Peking (see List of Gardens)   38, 126, 140, 142.

Xunzi (315-236 B.C.), Confucianist philosopher who considered man to be fundamentally ill-natured. With him originates the School of Legalists   80.

Yamato, great plain of the Kyōto-Nara region, where Japanese civilization originated   156.

Yiheyuan, Summer Palace, Peking (see List of Gardens)   18, 30, 36, 42, 46, 66-68, 70-72, 130, 143, 146, 148.

Yin and Yang, the two contradictory and complementary principles keeping the balance of the Universe, according to Chinese thought   21, 25, 30, 33, 35, 36, 39, 45, 50, 51, 55, 64, 99, 108, 113, 119, 166, 181.

Yingzhou, one of the three mythical Isles of the Immortals located in the Gulf of Bohai   140.

Yiyuan, Garden of Harmony, Suzhou (see List of Gardens)   99, 139, 157.

You Qiu (16th century), Ming painter, son-in-law of the master Qiu Ying. Considered a good figure painter, but rather conservative   83.

Yu the Great, successor of the five mythical rulers and founder of the Xia dynasty (c. 2200-1800 B.C.)   59, 66.

Yuan dynasty (1276-1368), following the Song and preceding the Ming. The first foreign (Mongol) dynasty, with Peking as capital   75, 110, 124, 175, 189, 192.

Yuan Jiang, Qing painter   84.

229

Yuhuayuan, Imperial Garden, Peking (see List of Gardens) 21, 37-41, 98, 107, 136, 146.

Yu Jian, Southern Song painter. In the early Yuan period, Chan monks fleeing Manchu domination and continuing the Song tradition took refuge in Japan, where they introduced a typically Chinese style of painting. No less than four late Song and early Yuan painters bear the name Yu Jian. The one referred to is either Yu Jian Ruo Fen, a Buddhist monk of the Tiantai sect (Tendai in Japanese), or Ying Yu Jian, a monk of the Chan sect. "Rather than assuming that late Sung art came into being under the influence of Zen Buddhism, should we not, perhaps, think of Zen painting as proof of the complete acceptance of Chinese aesthetics by the last—and least Indian—of the Buddhist sects in China?" (Max Loer) 172, 178.

Yunnan province, south-west China, bounded on the north by Tibet and Sichuan, on the east by Gizhou and Guangxi, on the south by Vietnam and Laos, on the west by Burma 27.

Zeami (1365-1443), Japanese actor and playwright, author of a secret treatise on the Nō theatre (see Bibliography) 204, 209.

Zhang Ruoai (1713-1746), Qing painter of Tongcheng (Anhui province), son of the famous Qing painter Zhang Tingyu 92.

Zhan Ziqian (A.D. 551-604), Sui and early Tang painter, regarded as the first "realistic" landscapist 61.

Zhongshan Park (Sun Yat-sen Memorial), Peking (see List of Gardens) 40, 121, 122, 142, 151.

Zhou (c. 1027-256 B.C.), third and last kingdom of China, after that of the still legendary Xia. Over a thousand years later came the Northern Zhou (A.D. 557-581) and the Later Zhou (951-960), just before the Song dynasty 80.

Zhou Chen (1450-1535), Ming painter born at Suzhou. In the Manchu period he looked to the past and followed in the wake of the Song masters 122, 128.

Zhou Wenju (10th century), Southern Tang painter 116.

Zhuangzi (c. 350-270 B.C.), one of the greatest philosophers of the Taoist school, author of the *Zhuangzi*. He saw the only salvation in a return to a primitive age when man lived in harmony with himself and nature. By an inner stripping away, one reverts inwardly to the universal movement of Tao and, by merging with it, loses all individual consciousness. Then, say the Taoists, the body becomes light, floats on the wind, feeds on dew and lives thousands of years. Zhuangzi is recognized as the greatest writer of ancient China 82.

Zhuozhengyuan, Garden of the Stupid Official, Suzhou (see List of Gardens) 24.

Zong Bing (A.D. 375-443), a native of Nanyang (Henan province). After passing the civil examinations, he refused any official post and preferred, with his like-minded wife, to live a bohemian life devoted to the arts. With Wang Wei the Elder (415-443), he was one of the first great theorists of Chinese painting but his works are lost 118, 119.

Zuiho-in, Kyōto (see List of Gardens) 10, 11, 157.

ACKNOWLEDGMENTS

The authors are grateful to many people for help received in the making of this book. Their thanks go first of all to Mr. Jurg PFRÜNDER, who travelled with them in China and gave them the benefit of his thorough knowledge of the Chinese language, culture and society; and to Mr. Georges GOORMAGHTIGH, Lecturer at the Arts School of the University of Geneva, who kindly read their manuscript and provided further information about the paintings and prints reproduced.

Their thanks are also due to the following: Mr. CHEN CONGZHOU, Professor of Architecture at Tongji University, Shanghai, a leading authority on Chinese gardens, who hospitably received them in Shanghai; Mr. Dominique DREYER, attaché at the Swiss Embassy in Peking, who spared no pains to smooth their way in China; Mr. Frank DUNAND, Curator of the Baur Collections of Oriental art in Geneva, who permitted them to publish two rare pieces; Mr. MA CHENGYUAN, Chief Curator of the Shanghai Museum, who provided photographs of the paintings they wished to reproduce; Mr. Renaud NEUBAUER of the Institute of Oriental Studies in Geneva, for several translations; Mrs. Janette OSTIER and Mrs. Nelly DELAY of Paris, who provided photographs of works in their keeping; Mr. Pierre RYCKMANS, the eminent Belgian sinologist, who gave them permission to quote freely from his translation of and commentary on Shitao's *Remarks on Painting*; Mr. Pierre-Francis SCHNEEBERGER, former Curator of the Baur Collections in Geneva, for permission to publish his essay on dragons; Mr. Jean-Marie SIMONET, Scientific Director of the Belgian Institute of Higher Chinese Studies, who permitted them to quote a passage from one of his lectures; Mr. WANG JINFU, Assistant Curator of the Old Imperial Palace Museum in Peking, who permitted them to photograph the gardens of the Forbidden City, which are still closed to the public, and provided them with some rare photographs of paintings.

Editorial director: Lauro Venturi

Text and illustrations printed by
IRL Imprimeries Réunies Lausanne s.a.
Binding by
Mayer et Soutter, Renens–Lausanne

Library of Congress Cataloging-in-Publication Data

Rambach, Pierre, 1925–
   Gardens of longevity in China and Japan.

   Translation of: Les jardins de longévité:
l'art des dresseurs de pierres en Chine et au Japon.
   Bibliography: p.
   Includes index.
   1. Rock gardens, Chinese. 2. Rock gardens, Japanese. 3. Gardens, Chinese.
4. Gardens, Japanese. 5. Gardens—China. 6. Gardens—Japan.
I. Rambach, Suzanne. II. Title.
SB457.55.R3613 1987   717   87-9671
ISBN 0-8478-0837-8

Printed in Switzerland